VEGAN

FAST FOOD

COPYCAT BURGERS, TACOS, FRIED CHICKEN, MILKSHAKES, AND MORE!

BRIAN WATSON
AKA THEE BURGER DUDE

HARVARD
COMMON
PRESS

First Published in 2022 by The Harvard Common Press, an imprint of The Quarto Group, 100 Cummings Center, Suite 265-D, Beverly, MA 01915, USA.

T (978) 282-9590 F (978) 283-2742 Quarto.com

26 25 24 23 22   1 2 3 4 5

ISBN: 978-0-7603-7585-3

Digital edition published in 2022

eISBN: 978-0-7603-7586-0

Library of Congress Cataloging-in-Publication Data is available

Design, Cover Image, and Page Layout: Mattie Wells

Photography: Brian Watson

Printed in USA
Printed in China

DEDICATION

In loving memory of my cat, Pixel, the best sous-
chef I've ever had. He was by my side every moment
during the creation of this book, meowing at me in
the kitchen to show his support and encouragement.
He changed the way I view animals and had a
tremendous effect on me. I think about him every
day and I hope he knew how much I loved him.
I miss you little buddy.

CONTENTS

INTRODUCTION

Hey, everybody! I'm Brian Watson, aka Thee Burger Dude. Suffice to say if you had told my former self that I'd be writing a vegan cookbook, I would've died laughing. I was always a big fan of burgers, fried chicken, mac 'n' cheese, pizza, burritos, you name it! I'm pretty sure nearly every meal I ate had some kind of meat drenched in some kind of dairy product. Perhaps I'd skip meat once in a while to be "healthy," but it was a huge part of my diet.

That being said, I wasn't super stoked on how we treated animals . . . but I just really loved meat. I assumed it was a necessary evil, and to be honest, I often avoided thinking about the whole thing altogether.

Plus when I imagined vegan food, it was boring and bland! It was basically just salads to me. Turns out, I had a very dated and stereotypical view of vegans as rich, trust-fund hippies who lived off of eating grass and their own moral superiority. (Well, okay, those vegans do exist, but thankfully they are not the majority!)

Eventually more vegan and plant-based products made their way onto my radar. I had tried some in the past, but they were awful. The new ones were different. Many were close enough that I felt like I could stop eating certain animal products. I began to cook with them and experiment with new ingredients I had never even heard of. (What the heck is nooch?) I even started to eat more vegetables, and I liked most of them! Strange things were afoot, but in a good way.

On top of that, I started to educate myself on the meat and dairy industries, plus the clothing, cosmetic, and entertainment industries that exploit animals. I realized and appreciated that all animals can feel pain and terror, or joy and happiness. They are just like our companion dogs and cats. And I knew that I had to adjust my actions accordingly.

On New Year's Eve 2018, I resolved to go vegan by the end of the year. Well, it only took until March—I went vegan nine months early! I quickly dove into making vegan food, and soon enough, I was trying to figure out ways to make all my old fast-food and comfort-food favorites.

I started off making lots of burgers—I know weird right! I was posting them on my personal Instagram account, and I was super excited about these new vegan burgers and wanted to get my friends to try them out. My wife suggested I start an Instagram account solely for my food posts. This was something that I didn't know existed. I looked into it and thought, "Sure, what's the worst that could happen!"

It took off, and soon people started asking me for recipes for the things I was posting. I went ahead and started up a recipe blog. Then, folks asked for videos for some of the techniques, so I started a YouTube channel! And now I'm lucky enough to write a cookbook.

Anyways, the whole point of my blog, YouTube channel, and this cookbook is simple: For the curious non-vegans out there—like me before I went vegan—I want to help you see that you can still have all of your favorite foods. Burgers, fried chicken, mac 'n' cheese, milkshakes, or whatever you like—it can all be totally plant-based! I also hope to help my fellow longtime vegans who are missing some of their old favorites (or who never got to try a certain fast-food order).

Maybe you need a full recipe from start to finish. Or maybe you've cracked the code to quite a bit on your own. Maybe you just need a few tricks or tips to take your recipe from good to great. If so, I hope this book has just what you've been looking for!

VEGAN

KITCHEN

& DELI

CHAPTER 1

BURGER BASICS

In most ways, a vegan burger (meaning the whole sandwich, not just the patty!) is exactly like a non-vegan burger. All we need to do is swap the ingredients that aren't vegan. But there is a bit of nuance to a vegan burger, so let's go over each component.

Buns

A lot of folks ask me where I get my buns. In my experience, many ready-made buns are vegan. In fact, in some stores most of them are. I always check the ingredients for eggs, butter, milk (including whey and casein), honey, etc. But unless it's brioche, Hawaiian, or honey wheat, there's a good chance it's vegan. I've even found brioche and Hawaiian without any animal products in them, so it never hurts to check.

There are ingredients, such as mono-diglycerides, DATEM, and others, that may or may not be plant-based. But from my understanding, they usually are. I don't worry about these ingredients, but if you do, contact the manufacturer and enquire about them. You might also see "May Contain Milk" on the packaging. This simply means that the product was made in a facility that also produces non-vegan food. It doesn't mean the product actually has milk in it; it's just a warning for folks with dairy allergies.

And obviously, you can always make your own buns if you prefer!

To prepare burger buns, two things are important: First, you should always toast or grill your buns, usually with a bit of vegan butter or oil, until golden brown. This improves the texture, and it helps keep your buns from getting soggy. Second, if you toast your buns, let them rest on a wire rack. If you just set them on a plate, they'll steam and get soggy. This will ruin your burger before you even get the patty on there!

Cheese

Vegan cheese has come a long way in the past few years. There are plenty of options these days, so I recommend trying a bunch and figuring out what you like best. For most burgers, I prefer American slices. When preparing your burger, I highly recommend adding a little water to the pan and covering it to melt the cheese on your patty. There's not much sadder than unmelted cheese on a cheeseburger!

Toppings

There are nearly endless toppings you can put on a burger, and everyone has their own preferences. I like to keep things simple: It's hard to beat a cheeseburger with some burger sauce, pickles, and onions. If I could eat only one burger the rest of my life, that would be it!

Piling on too many toppings can result in a burger that is difficult to eat. (I speak from experience.) It will fall apart and get soggy, plus the flavors and textures of all the toppings will clash. You can always wrap your burger in some deli paper to keep it from going all over the place, but it's worth it to be mindful of how the toppings will accent and complement each other.

Patties

Last but not least, the main event! There have been a lot of advances in vegan burger meat over the past few years with companies such as Beyond Meat, Impossible, and the like. The burgers are packaged to look like ground beef, and they taste the closest to ground beef—especially when compared to "last generation" veggie burgers.

The burgers typically cook like animal-based burgers. The main difference I've noticed is they don't shrink, so you don't need to make a dimple in your burger patty. They tend to dry out if you make the patties too thin, especially when making a smash burger or grilling outdoors on the BBQ. Keeping the patties about ½" (13 mm) thick will help ensure a perfectly cooked burger that's still juicy!

For pan-grilling, I use nonstick, cast-iron, or carbon steel pans. They all work great, so use whatever you are comfortable with. Nonstick is the best for beginners as you won't have to worry about your burgers sticking to the pan!

I prefer to form my patties by pressing them down by hand onto some parchment paper. I recommend doing so inside a cookie cutter, about 3½ to 4½ inches (9 to 11 cm) as a guide. Of course a burger press works great, too!

Making burgers from scratch is also an option. I have two recipes in this book (starting on page 14) for homemade burger patties if that floats your boat!

While my recipes and store-bought burgers may be to your taste, please always feel free to season your burgers as you see fit. Salt, pepper, paprika, garlic, and onion powder are great ways to amp up a burger. Experiment with it and have fun!

TVP/ SEITAN BURGER

These are some of the best homemade vegan burgers I've ever had, and its thanks in large part to textured vegetable protein (aka TVP). We'll also be adding some vital wheat gluten to give these burgers a nice meaty chew! This recipe is a good base to start with, but flavor them however you'd like. The burgers last for four to five days in the fridge, and they can be frozen for a few months. Cook them like you would any other burger. They are great on the grill, too!

YIELD: 4 TO 6 BURGERS

INGREDIENTS

Burgers
- 1 cup (100 g) TVP crumbles
- 1 cup (235 ml) beefless broth or veggie broth
- ½ cup (56 g) vital wheat gluten, plus more if needed
- ¼ cup (48 g) potato starch, plus more if needed
- 1 tablespoon (8 g) mushroom seasoning
- 1 teaspoon garlic powder
- 1 teaspoon onion powder
- 1 teaspoon smoked paprika
- 1 tablespoon (5 g) nutritional yeast
- 1 tablespoon (15 ml) soy sauce
- 2 tablespoons (28 ml) neutral oil
- 1 tablespoon (20 g) blackstrap molasses
- 1 tablespoon (16 g) tomato paste
- ½ teaspoon liquid smoke
- 1 teaspoon Marmite (optional)

Grilling and Serving
- Neutral oil for brushing
- Salt and pepper
- Toasted buns
- Toppings of your choice

INSTRUCTIONS

Making the Burgers

1. In a large bowl, rehydrate the TVP in the broth for 30 minutes. Once all liquid has been absorbed, prepare a pot with a steamer basket.

2. Combine all the ingredients in the bowl and knead in the vital wheat gluten until you can form a patty with the mixture. If a patty can be lightly tossed between your hands without falling apart, then it's good to go. If it's too mushy, add a little more vital wheat gluten or potato starch until it holds its shape. Conversely, if it's too dry, add a little water until it will stick together.

3. Form into 3- or 4-ounce (85- to 113-g) patties, using a cookie cutter to get them as round and even as possible. (You can also form them by hand.) Once all the patties are formed, wrap them individually in foil; wrap the patties in parchment paper first, if you want to avoid foil touching the food. Wrap them very tightly in the foil so they don't expand too much.

4. Steam the patties for 45 minutes.

5. Let them cool completely and store them in the refrigerator overnight.

Grilling the Burgers

The burgers are now ready for grilling! Brush them with a little oil to help them get nice and browned, and always season to taste with salt and pepper. Grill them like any other burger, for about 3 minutes per side over medium heat. Top them with some vegan cheese, cover, and steam to melt the cheese. Then, put a patty between two buns along with any desired toppings and enjoy!

OLD–
FASHIONED
BEAN
BURGER

I feel like the bean burger gets a bad rep, mostly because some of them are super bland! Well, if I had had one this good back in the '90s, I might've been a convert much earlier! I prefer pinto beans, but black beans will totally work for these, too. Drying the beans in the oven before assembling the patties will help keep these burgers from getting too mushy—the bane of countless vegan burgers' existence!

YIELD: 4 TO 6 BURGERS

INGREDIENTS

Burgers

- 2 cans (15 ounces, or 425 g each) pinto or black beans
- 1 tablespoon (14 g) ground flax plus 2 tablespoons (28 ml) water
- 3 tablespoons (21 g) bread crumbs, plus more if needed
- 2 tablespoons (16 g) cornstarch, plus more if needed
- ½ teaspoon onion powder
- 1 teaspoon garlic powder
- 1 teaspoon smoked paprika
- 1 tablespoon (5 g) nutritional yeast
- 1 tablespoon (8 g) mushroom seasoning
- 1 tablespoon (20 g) blackstrap molasses
- 1–2 tablespoons (15–28 ml) soy sauce
- 3 tablespoons (45 ml) neutral oil
- 1 tablespoon (16 g) diced chipotles in adobo
- ½ teaspoon liquid smoke
- Black pepper

Grilling and Serving

- Neutral oil for brushing
- Salt and pepper
- Toasted buns
- Toppings of your choice

INSTRUCTIONS

Making the Burgers

1. Preheat the oven to 350°F (175°C or gas mark 4). Drain and wash the canned beans, then lay them out on a parchment-lined baking sheet in a single layer. Bake for 15 minutes. Remove them from the oven and add to a food processor. Pulse 5 to 6 times until they are ground up into pieces similar to ground beef.

2. Make the flax egg by combining the flax and water in a small bowl. Let the mixture sit and thicken for 5 minutes. Next, add all the ingredients to a large bowl and mix thoroughly. Taste and adjust for seasoning.

3. Form 3- to 4-ounce (85- to 113-g) patties, using a cookie cutter so they are all uniform. (Forming by hand is fine, too!) If a patty can be lightly tossed between your hands without falling apart, then it's good to go. If it's too mushy, add a little more cornstarch or bread crumbs until it holds its shape. Conversely, if it's too dry, add a little water until it will stick together.

4. Refrigerate for at least 30 minutes before grilling.

Grilling the Burgers

The burgers are now ready for grilling! Brush them with a little oil to help them get nice and browned, and always season to taste with salt and pepper. Grill your burgers like any other burger, for about 3 minutes per side over medium heat. Top them with some vegan cheese, cover, and steam to melt the cheese. Then, put a patty between two buns along with any desired toppings and enjoy!

HOW TO GRILL BURGERS

Cooking plant-based burgers is similar to their animal counterparts, but like I've mentioned before, there are some slight differences. In order to cook plant-based burgers successfully, there are a few things we should go over! It's worth noting that these tips are mostly for the store-bought burgers that you'll find out there that mimic meat rather than homemade patties. The fat content makes it possible to get textures that truly mock meat.

NONSTICK PAN

SMASHBURGER

BBQ GRILL

Method 1: Smashburger

My new favorite way to cook patties is by making a smashburger. In case you aren't familiar, instead of forming a patty and throwing it in the skillet, we're going to take a ball of plant-based meat, place it in a ripping-hot cast-iron pan, then smash it with a strong metal spatula or burger iron. This creates the most surface contact with the pan possible, which will result in a beautifully browned and delicious crust on the burger. It's honestly one of the easiest ways to level up a patty once you get the hang of it.

However, the way that cooking this burger differs from an animal-based patty is that plant fat melts faster than animal fat, which means you risk drying out your patty before you get that seared crust. Traditionally, smashburgers are pretty flat and thin in order to get those crispy edges. When we do this with plant-based burgers, they get so dried out that it ruins the burger. But there is a simple fix for this: Just smash them so they're not quite as thin! After extensive testing, I suggest using a 4-ounce (114 g) ball of meat and smashing to about ½ inch (13 mm) thick. This way the patty will still stay juicy and you'll still get that perfect sear.

I highly recommend using a cast-iron pan. A carbon or stainless-steel pan will work, too, but don't use nonstick as it won't get hot enough and the burger won't adhere to the pan. For the spatula, make sure you are using a stiff, strong metal spatula for smashing, and for scraping the burger off the pan.

In order to cook this thing, get the pan smoking hot—there should literally be a small amount of smoke—then add some high smoke point oil (I like avocado oil). Smear the oil around a bit with your spatula, add the meat, smash, and then season with salt and pepper.

Cook that for about 2 minutes and flip when you see a dark brown crust forming. The patty will want to stick to the pan; use your spatula to pry it up and eventually it will loosen its grip. After that, you just need to add some vegan cheese, squirt some water in the pan, and cover to steam and melt the cheese. You should have a pretty perfect vegan smashburger!

Method 2: Nonstick Skillet

If the smashburger sounds too complicated, you can also cook it in a nonstick pan! This is definitely the easiest and most foolproof way to cook a burger, and it'll still be delicious! Just form a 3- to 4-ounce (85- to 114-g) patty to your desired size and cook it for 3–4 minutes per side over medium heat. That's it!

Method 3: BBQ Grill

Cooking these burgers on an outdoor BBQ grill is a great method as well as it will infuse some smoky flavor. The only thing you really need to keep in mind is just like with a smashburger, a thinner patty will dry out faster. So, keep your BBQ burger patties relatively thick—in this case, I'd say at least ½ inch (13 mm). Another tip is to get a folded up paper towel, dip it in a little cooking oil, then using tongs, oil up the grill grates. This will help keep the burger from sticking to the grill and will help get you those classic grill marks. I like to sear mine over high heat, but if the fat drippings cause flare-ups, make sure you have a cool spot on the grill to move it. Other than that, just cook it to your desired doneness and enjoy!

FRIED CHICK'N
BASICS

When you're making fried chicken for the recipes in this book, you're faced with three main variables. We'll run through each of them in this section. First, what is the "meat" you want to use? There are many good options, but chances are you'll find a favorite. Second, how are you going to batter it? If you're not using store-bought, pre-battered product, then you're going to have to dredge and batter. Last but not least, how are you frying it? While deep-fried will give you the most classic taste and texture, consider air-frying for a healthier (but still crispy!) option.

OYSTER MUSHROOMS

STORE-BOUGHT VEGAN CHICK'N

TWICE FROZEN TOFU

The Chick'n

STORE-BOUGHT

A lot of the options you can buy from the fridge or freezer section of the supermarket are subpar when it comes to breading. You might find a protein mix you like, but the batter just won't sing! Thus, if you can find some vegan chick'n products that aren't already breaded and fried, that's the ticket. I recommend letting them thaw and reshaping them however you'd like (patties, nuggets, tenders, etc.). Then, bread and fry them as you would for any other option that follows. This is what I usually do!

OYSTER MUSHROOMS

This is my second favorite option for fried chick'n. Oyster mushrooms have a great texture, and they also provide a lot of nooks and crannies for the dredging, which will give you an amazingly crispy chick'n! They do get a little chewy toward the stems, so be aware of that.

These mushrooms have a lot of clusters, and they can be broken up into smaller pieces to make nuggets or tenders. You should be able to find them at your local grocery store or at health food stores or Asian markets.

An important thing to note is that oyster mushrooms weigh much less than tofu or seitan and store-bought vegan chick'n, so keep that in mind! The photo above shows 5 ounces (142 g) of both oyster mushrooms and tofu, and 10 ounces (283 g) of a store-bought vegan chick'n.

TWICE FROZEN TOFU

Using tofu is pretty straightforward. For medium-firm tofu, simply freeze and thaw the tofu in its package twice: Freeze it, let it thaw, and then repeat. This process causes the water in the tofu to expand when it freezes. It will create a much more fibrous and "meat-like" texture. Once the tofu is thawed for the second time, press all the liquid out. It will be very delicate and want to break apart. Break it into pieces for nuggets or tenders; if you want to make patties, I suggest slicing it instead. When you have the patty shape, freeze it one last time so it won't fall apart when you dredge it. The larger the piece is, the more delicate it will be. I've also used this method successfully with extra-firm tofu, but some have found it to be too spongy, so keep that in mind.

If you want to do something faster, super-firm tofu is quick and easy because it doesn't need to be pressed at all. Simply cut or tear off pieces, and then dredge and fry it like you would any other vegan chick'n. Just note the texture will be more dense.

SEITAN

Seitan can make great fried chick'n. There are many varieties of store-bought seitan, I've seen it in most of the major big box stores, specialty stores, and it's widely available in most Asian markets, too! You can also make your own at home if you wish.

It's worth noting that seitan is not for those with a gluten allergy or intolerance as it's basically pure gluten!

Batter

Frying vegan chick'n is nearly identical to frying regular chicken, but with one simple swap: We'll be ditching the buttermilk/eggs and using plant-based milk and vinegar! The vinegar will curdle and thicken the plant milk, and it will work as an excellent binder for the flour mixture. I recommend using a high-protein plant milk as it will curdle and thicken better. If the buttermilk is too thin, your breading may come out flat.

I need to stress the importance of using *unsweetened* plant milk for this. I can still remember the one time I accidentally bought a vanilla-flavored milk and after all that work, I bit into a really weird tasting piece of fried chick'n! I've recently started adding a little flour to the vegan buttermilk mixture as well, and I've found that it lends a lighter, crispier crunch, too!

Most recipes in this book have their own seasoned flour mixture. This is where we're going to get a lot of our flavor. There are endless ways to do this, but salt, garlic and onion powders, smoked paprika, black and white peppers, and cayenne pepper are all great additions.

In most cases I use a 1:1 ratio of flour and cornstarch. For every 1 cup (120 g) of that mixture, I add 1 tablespoon (14 g) of baking powder. Baking powder is essential for a crispy, crunchy fried chick'n. And on top of that I add 2 to 3 tablespoons of seasoning.

Dredging

Typically, I will double dredge the vegan chick'n: coat first in the wet, then the dry, then the wet again, then the dry again. The exception is a buttermilk mixture that's had a little flour added to it. For this, I've found that going first to dry, then to wet, and then back again to dry gets pretty outstanding results. Just remember to shake off the excess flour and allow the wet batter to drip off the excess, as this will help with the final product!

You can also fry with bread crumbs: Start dredging with the flour mixture, then the wet, and finish with the bread crumbs. Note: Some recipes may call for a double dredge first to the flour, then the wet, then bread crumbs, and then back to the wet, and one last dredge in the bread crumbs again.

TOFU

OYSTER MUSHROOMS

STORE-BOUGHT VEGAN CHICK'N

Frying

Last but not least: the frying itself! There are a few ways to go about this. More often than not, I fry in peanut oil in a large saucepan or Dutch oven between 350° and 375°F (175° to 190°C). A large, cast-iron skillet works great, too; it can retain heat and it likely has a wider surface area. I realize deep frying can be scary to somebody who's never done it. With some careful planning and know-how, those fears can be abated, and you can be a master in no time!

AIR-FRYING

Making vegan fried chick'n in the air fryer is a great alternative if you don't want to deal with the oil that's necessary for deep frying. To air-fry the fried chick'n recipes, I recommend lining the air fryer with parchment paper: I use a chopstick to poke a few holes in the parchment. It's important to preheat the air fryer *without* the parchment so it doesn't fly around and possibly catch on fire.

Dredge the chick'n according to the recipe's instructions, and spray it with a little cooking spray. Line the air fryer with the parchment and arrange the chick'n on it. Be careful not to crowd the air fryer.

Air-fry the chick'n at 375°F (190°C) for 6 minutes, flip, and spray them again. Then, simply repeat the process until they are golden brown. This typically takes three to four rounds, about 18 to 24 minutes.

DEEP-FRYING SAFETY TIPS

Here are some good rules and tips to ensure a safe and successful deep-frying experience.

→ **Oil:** Use oils with high smoke points, so they don't burn or catch on fire. I like peanut the best; vegetable or canola oil is fine, too. Don't use olive oil!

→ **Thermometer:** Use a deep-fry or candy thermometer. This will help you make sure the oil doesn't get too hot, and help you cook your food at the correct temperature.

→ **Plan ahead:** Don't fill your skillet or pot more than halfway with oil. And don't crowd the pan either!

→ **Handle placement:** Turn the handle of the pot *away* from you. This way you won't accidentally hit it or push it down and cause the oil to spill.

→ **Lid:** Keep a lid nearby. If the oil does catch on fire, immediately cover it with a lid or large baking sheet. Never throw water on an oil fire!

→ **No water:** Speaking of water, don't put anything wet into the hot oil. Sometimes we might have a wet batter, like a tempura, but try not to get any water in there. This goes for the utensils, too. Avoid washing them while you are deep frying as even a tiny bit of water can create chaos inside hot oil.

→ **Keep your distance:** When adding food to the oil by hand, always do so carefully: let it gently fall away from you, so it doesn't splash any hot oil on your hands or arms. Always use long tongs or a slotted spoon/spider to remove food.

→ **Clean up:** When you are done frying, turn off the heat and let the oil cool down completely. Also, don't throw away used oil! Strain it through a fine-mesh strainer lined with a paper towel and save it. Oil can usually be reused three to four times depending on what you fry with it.

UNDERDONE **PERFECTLY FRIED** **OVERDONE**

KITCHEN GEAR AND INGREDIENTS

Assuming you have the basics, such as pots, pans, spatulas, and other commonly used utensils, here's a list of more specialized items that have made my life in the kitchen a whole lot easier. Make a few recipes, and then decide for yourself what to buy.

Melting Domes: I've found that smaller melting domes will melt the cheese much faster and more effectively than a pot lid. As we all know, vegan cheese doesn't like to melt, so any help we can get is a good thing!

Cookie Cutters: I used to use a burger press to form my patties, but now I prefer a set of cookie cutters. Having options is good, because your patties may need to be different sizes depending on the size of your buns. Also, they are super handy for things like biscuits . . . and obviously cookies.

Thermometer: Frying at the correct temperature is crucial for deep frying, so in my opinion, a thermometer is mandatory in order to get perfect results.

Spider Spoons and Strainers: These come in handy for a multitude of reasons, and they are essential for getting food out of your hot, deep-fry oil!

Wire Rack: Freshly toasted burger buns and anything fried, such as chick'n or French fries, will benefit from wire racks. They create better airflow and help ensure your food doesn't get soggy as it cools down.

Air Fryer: If you don't want to deep fry because of the oil or cleanup, this is a great alternative! An air fryer is convenient, and most brands will give you good results! I've found the air fryer to be great for reheating things that used to be crispy.

High-Speed Blender: I use this for all sorts of things, but what made me buy one in the first place was making vegan cheeses and ice cream. This tool will absolutely pulverize any kind of nut and you won't need to strain out any chunky bits.

Stand Mixer: For making dough, this thing is indispensable! Your arms will thank you!

Food Scale: This is especially good for weighing ingredients (such as flour), and it's just good to have when you need to be precise about anything!

Lemon Juicer: I can't count how many times I used to squeeze a lemon or lime through my hands to catch the seeds, but no more!

Seasoning Shakers: If you are going to make your own seasoning mixes, having shakers is a must!

Fry Cutter: Cutting fries by hand is okay, but if you have the space for it, a French fry press is ideal.

Squeeze Bottles: Obviously, you can just use some plastic container and a spoon to get your condiments on your burger. But squeeze bottles give you the full fast-food experience.

Funnels: Speaking of squeeze bottles, getting your homemade sauces into the squeeze bottles will be difficult and messy without a funnel or two.

(UN)COMMON INGREDIENTS

Sodium Citrate: This is a common emulsifier used in cheese sauces. It helps to ensure a smooth and velvety cheese experience!

Lactic Acid: This will impart a very distinct "tang" to cheese and other dishes. You can sub with vinegar or lemon juice, but I find that lactic acid has its own superior quality that can't be matched. Not all lactic acid is vegan, so make sure to check.

Nutritional Yeast: This is a vegan staple; it's used in many dishes to impart a "cheesy" umami-type flavor. It's great in many applications beyond vegan cheese!

Smoked Paprika: I use this all the time! If you like things spicy and smoky, pick it up.

Chipotles in Adobo: Much like smoked paprika, chopped chipotles in adobo make everything taste smokier! I prefer using a jar of pre-diced chiles because I can easily use a tablespoon when I need it.

Beefless Broth: Some kind of beefless broth powder or paste is indispensable when making any vegan meat. You can always use veggie broth instead, but it will lack that "beefy" flavor. This also goes for any vegan chicken broth—same idea! You should be able to find this at your local Asian market or online.

Blackstrap Molasses: Alongside the beefless broth, blackstrap molasses will make things taste beefier as well. In fact, if you can't find any beefless broth, using some veggie broth with a mixture of blackstrap molasses and vegan Worcestershire sauce can roughly approximate it.

Mushroom Seasoning: You can find this at your local Asian market or online. It will enhance the umami factor of any dish you use it in.

Soy Curls™: Soy Curls are simply dehydrated soybeans formed into curl-like shapes. They are one of my favorite products, and they are magical! Use them for any kind of meat dish with chopped meat. They are unflavored and absorb any marinade you cook them in, so you can flavor them to taste more like beef or chicken. They work great in the Kung Pao Chicken (page 90) or the Burrito Bowl (page 84).

TVP: Short for textured vegetable protein, TVP is very similar to Soy Curls, but varies in shape and size. I use the smaller ones for ground beef or in vegan burger patties (page 14). The larger "chunks" and "slices" can be used in a million ways!

Flax "Egg": This is what I often use to replace an egg in vegan recipes. It's just 1 tablespoon (14 g) of ground flax combined with 2 to 3 tablespoons (28 to 45 ml) of water. It works great and has a fairly neutral taste, making it my go-to for baking or as a binding ingredient. Note: This won't replicate an egg the way that say a tofu scramble will mimic scrambled eggs!

RICE PAPER BACON

I've made a lot of vegan bacon, and this is by far my favorite. I've found that it's the easiest, fastest, and most foolproof bacon—and the taste and texture are fantastic! I make a big batch, store the leftovers in the fridge, and reheat them for a sandwich or burger. I like to fry the slices, so they are crispy on the edges and slightly chewy in the middle. They will crisp up a bit after frying, so keep that in mind! I recommend cooking a few test pieces to figure out what kind of texture you like.

YIELD: 18 TO 24 SLICES

INGREDIENTS

Marinade

- 2 tablespoons (28 ml) neutral oil (vegetable or refined coconut oil works well)
- 3 tablespoons (45 ml) soy sauce or tamari
- 1 teaspoon liquid smoke
- 1 tablespoon (20 g) maple syrup

- 1 teaspoon sriracha
- 2 tablespoons (10 g) nutritional yeast
- 1 teaspoon MSG or mushroom seasoning
- 1 teaspoon garlic powder
- 1 teaspoon smoked paprika

Rice Paper Bacon

- 6–8 pieces of rice paper
- Neutral oil for cooking

INSTRUCTIONS

Marinade

Combine all the ingredients for the marinade in a small bowl. Taste for seasoning. It will be strong and salty. Don't worry! Each strip of bacon will only have a small amount of the marinade, so it won't be as intense.

Rice Paper Bacon

1. Transfer the marinade to a large, rimmed plate or skillet. Add some water to another large, rimmed plate or skillet. Take two pieces of the rice paper and gently coat them in water for about 15 seconds, or until they begin to soften. This is to rehydrate them and make them pliable; they'll continue to rehydrate after they are removed from the water. Gently press them together and try to remove any air bubbles. Add the rice paper bacon sheets to the marinade and coat both sides.

2. Place the rice paper on the cutting board, being careful not to let the rice paper fold onto itself. Seal off the edges so there are no air bubbles. A pastry brush can help get out the bubbles and distribute the marinade evenly.

3. Using a knife or pizza cutter, slice the rice paper into bacon strips, about 1 to 1½ inches (2.5 to 3.5 cm) wide. Place the strips on a wire rack and repeat until all the strips are sliced and ready to fry.

Frying

Bring a 12-inch (30-cm) skillet up to medium heat. Add enough frying oil to coat the entire pan and then add a little more. Once the oil is heated up, fry the strips to the desired doneness. Let them cool on a wire rack. Serve immediately. You can also store the strips in an airtight container for 2 to 3 days or refrigerate for 2 to 3 weeks.

TVP GROUND BEEF

This is a highly versatile and relatively inexpensive option for ground beef. It can be swapped in just about any application that calls for ground beef. Try it in the Mexican Pizza (page 70), Crunchwrap Supreme (page 66), and the Chili Cheese Tots (page 100).

YIELD: 6 TO 8 SERVINGS

INGREDIENTS

Beef
- 1 cup (100 g) TVP crumbles
- 1½ cups (355 ml) beefless broth

Marinade
- ¾ cup (175 ml) beefless broth
- 1 tablespoon (16 g) tomato paste
- 1 teaspoon onion powder
- 1 teaspoon smoked paprika
- 1 teaspoon garlic powder
- 1 teaspoon nutritional yeast
- 1 teaspoon vegan Worcestershire sauce
- 1 tablespoon (20 g) blackstrap molasses
- Salt and pepper
- 1 teaspoon MSG (optional)

INSTRUCTIONS

Rehydrate

Soak the TVP in the beefless broth for 30 minutes, or until all the liquid has been absorbed.

Ground Beef

To turn the TVP into vegan ground beef, combine the TVP with all the marinade ingredients in a large skillet over medium heat. Cook for 5 minutes, or until nearly all the liquid has been absorbed and reduced.

VERSATILE VITTLES

This TVP Ground Beef can also be used in a bunch of different ways outside of the recipes for this book. I've used it for sloppy Joes, Bolognese, lasagna, stuffed peppers, stir-fries, you name it! It tastes great on its own but can be elevated in a bevy of ways, so let your imagination run wild and have fun with it!

CHEESE SAUCE

Cheese sauce is incredibly easy to make vegan! Following are two recipes: one that uses store-bought shredded vegan cheese, and one that is a cashew-based sauce. I love them both, but the cashew-based sauce does take longer to make. If you want something quick and easy, the store-bought cheese is the way to go! This sauce can be used for cheese fries, mac 'n' cheese, nachos—you name it.

If your Easy Cheese Sauce needs a flavor boost, feel free to add any seasonings you like. Garlic powder, onion powder, and smoked paprika are all good choices.

YIELD: 4 TO 6 SERVINGS

EASY CHEESE SAUCE

- ▶ 4 ounces (118 ml) water
- ▶ ½ teaspoon sodium citrate
- ▶ 8 ounces (226 g) shredded vegan cheddar cheese
- ▶ 1 tablespoon (8 g) tapioca starch
- ▶ Salt

Add the water to a medium saucepan and bring it to a boil. Add the sodium citrate and stir to dissolve. Add the vegan cheese and tapioca starch. Whisk until melted and smooth.

NOTE: Instead of sodium citrate, simply whisk in unsweetened plant milk in ¼-cup (60-ml) increments until the cheese sauce is smooth and velvety.

CASHEW-BASED SAUCE

- ▶ 4 cups (940 ml) water
- ▶ ½ cup (68 g) raw cashews
- ▶ 2 medium carrots, peeled and chopped
- ▶ 1½ cups (355 ml) unsweetened plant milk
- ▶ ¼ cup (20 g) nutritional yeast
- ▶ ½ teaspoon garlic powder
- ▶ ½ teaspoon onion powder
- ▶ ½ teaspoon ground turmeric
- ▶ ½ teaspoon smoked paprika
- ▶ ½ teaspoon mustard powder
- ▶ ½ teaspoon lactic acid, or to taste
- ▶ Salt

1. In a medium saucepot, bring the water up to a rolling boil. Place the cashews into a sturdy bowl, pour in enough boiling water to cover them, and let them soak for 10 to 15 minutes. While the cashews soak, return the pot to the stove, add the carrots, and cook them until fork-tender.

2. Add all the remaining ingredients to a high-speed blender. When the carrots and cashews are ready, add them to the blender. Blend until smooth. Taste and adjust for seasoning.

AMERICAN CHEESE HACK

To make an American cheese that has a superior melt, add the Easy Cheese Sauce to a square silicone mold and then freeze it. Let it partially thaw, and you can slice it or grate it! This is how I got the cheese to melt so well on my Mexican Pizza (page 70)!

CONDIMENTS

These are my top three dipping sauces and condiments! They are the most versatile and delicious in my book (figuratively and literally).

Store-bought BBQ sauce is often already vegan, as usually it's just honey or anchovies (via Worcestershire sauce) you need to watch out for. However, I much prefer a homemade sauce! It just tastes better, and you can tailor it to your own preferences. Same with the vegan ranch and honey mustard! For the "honey," use whatever you like as a sweetener. I've found that maple syrup, date syrup, and agave work great.

VEGAN HONEY MUSTARD

YIELD: SCANT 1 CUP (235 G)

- ½ cup (115 g) vegan mayo
- 2 tablespoons (30 g) Dijon mustard
- 2 tablespoons (22 g) yellow mustard
- 2 tablespoons (40 g) vegan honey (maple syrup, date syrup, or agave)
- 1 tablespoon (15 ml) lemon juice

In a small bowl, combine everything and refrigerate for at least 1 hour.

BBQ SAUCE

YIELD: 1¾ CUPS (420 G)

- 1 cup (240 g) ketchup
- ⅓ cup (80 ml) vinegar
- ½ cup (115 g) packed brown sugar
- 2 tablespoons (28 ml) hot sauce
- 2 teaspoons (10 ml) vegan Worcestershire
- 1 tablespoon (7 g) smoked paprika
- 1 teaspoon garlic powder
- Salt and pepper

Add everything to a saucepan over medium-high heat and bring to a light boil. Then, reduce the heat and simmer for 10 minutes.

VEGAN RANCH

YIELD: ¾ CUPS (175 G)

- ¼ cup (60 g) vegan mayo
- ¼ cup (60 g) vegan sour cream, store-bought or homemade (page 86)
- ¼ cup (60 ml) unsweetened plant milk
- ½ teaspoon dried dill
- ¼ teaspoon dried parsley
- ¼ teaspoon dried chives
- ¼ teaspoon salt
- ¼ teaspoon garlic powder
- ¼ teaspoon onion powder
- ¼ teaspoon lactic acid
- Black pepper

In a small bowl, combine everything and refrigerate for at least 1 hour.

BURGER SAUCE

To be honest, when I make burger sauce at home, I never measure anything. I typically eyeball and season to taste. This is a pretty good replication of what I make, and I can guarantee it'll go great on your next burger! Try it on sandwiches, grilled cheese, or as a fry dipping sauce! Feel free to tailor to your taste!

YIELD: ABOUT ¾ CUP (175 G)

- ▶ ½ cup (115 g) vegan mayo
- ▶ 2 tablespoons (30 g) ketchup
- ▶ 1 tablespoon (15 g) dill or sweet relish
- ▶ ½ tablespoon (8 g) Dijon mustard
- ▶ 1–2 teaspoons (5–10 ml) vinegar
- ▶ ¼ teaspoon garlic powder
- ▶ ¼ teaspoon onion powder
- ▶ ¼ teaspoon smoked paprika
- ▶ ⅛ teaspoon chipotle powder
- ▶ Salt and pepper

In a small bowl, combine everything and refrigerate for at least 1 hour.

TACO SEASONING

Store-bought taco seasoning is ubiquitous, however, like most things, the homemade version is much better. I love always having this handy so I can whip up some tacos or burritos whenever I get that hankering, which is quite often!

YIELD: ⅔ CUP (75 G)

- ▶ 3 tablespoons (23 g) chili seasoning
- ▶ 1 tablespoon (7 g) garlic powder
- ▶ 1 tablespoon (7 g) onion powder
- ▶ 1 tablespoon (7 g) ground cumin
- ▶ 1 tablespoon (7 g) smoked paprika
- ▶ 1 tablespoon (8 g) chipotle powder
- ▶ 1 tablespoon (3 g) dried oregano
- ▶ 2 teaspoons (4 g) ground coriander
- ▶ 1 teaspoon salt
- ▶ 1 teaspoon citric acid (optional but recommended!)

Combine everything in a seasoning shaker.

NOTE: Chili seasoning is an American mixed seasoning, not to be confused with a simple powder like a cayenne pepper powder. I usually use the McCormick brand.

BURGERS & CHICK'N

SANDWICHES

CHAPTER 2

40

**MCDONALD'S
BIG MAC®**

42

**BURGER KING
WHOPPER**

46

**IN-N-OUT BURGER
DOUBLE-DOUBLE®
ANIMAL STYLE®**

50

**WHATABURGER
PATTY MELT**

52

**WENDY'S
BACONATOR®**

54

**WHITE CASTLE
THE ORIGINAL SLIDER®**

56

**BURGER KING
ORIGINAL CHICKEN
SANDWICH**

58

**CHICK-FIL-A
CHICKEN SANDWICH**

60

**WHATABURGER
BUFFALO RANCH
CHICKEN STRIP
SANDWICH**

62

**KFC
NASHVILLE HOT
CHICKEN SANDWICH**

MCDONALD'S
BIG MAC®

Arguably the most recognizable fast-food burger in the world, this one hardly needs an introduction. Growing up, I LOVED these. I harassed my parents at least once a week to go get one. However, as I got older, I'm not sure if my taste buds changed, or if the quality went downhill, or both, but I hardly ever indulged in one. This homemade version is better than I remember from my youth, and since I'm an adult now, I can make it whenever I want.

YIELD: 4 BURGERS (PLUS EXTRA SAUCE)

INGREDIENTS

Sauce

- 1 cup (225 g) vegan mayo
- ¼ cup (60 g) ketchup
- 2 tablespoons (22 g) yellow mustard
- 2 tablespoons (30 g) sweet relish
- 1 teaspoon onion powder
- 1 teaspoon garlic powder
- ½ teaspoon smoked paprika
- 1 tablespoon (15 ml) white vinegar

Burgers

- 1 pound (454 g) plant-based meat (or use a homemade burger, page 30)
- 4 seeded hamburger buns plus 4 bottom buns (for the club bun)
- Neutral oil or vegan butter for cooking
- Salt and pepper
- 8 slices vegan cheese

Assembly

- 2 cups (110 g) shredded lettuce
- ½ cup (64 g) finely diced onion
- Dill pickle slices

NOTE: 2-ounce (57-g) patties are true to the original, but feel free to make them bigger if you'd like!

INSTRUCTIONS

Sauce

Combine everything in a small bowl or plastic container, and store in the fridge until needed.

Burgers

1. Form eight (2-ounce, or 57-g) patties from the plant-based meat using a burger press or cookie cutter.

2. To prepare the middle or club bun, use a serrated knife to shave off the very bottom of the bun to expose the interior.

3. Bring a pan up to medium heat with a little oil or vegan butter. Toast the buns and set them aside. Add the burger patties to the pan, and season to taste with salt and pepper. Cook for 3 to 4 minutes, or until browned.

4. Flip the patties, then add a slice of vegan cheese to each patty. Add a little water to the pan, then cover immediately to steam and melt the cheese, about 3 minutes.

Assembly

On the bottom bun, slather on some of the sauce, then top with some lettuce and onion. Add the first burger patty and the club bun. Then add more sauce, lettuce, and pickles followed by the second burger patty. Top with more onions and sauce, then the top bun, and ENJOY!

BURGER KING WHOPPER

When I was nineteen years old, it was the year I lived off Whoppers. They had a special back then and they were only 99¢! So, for a broke kid trying to make it as a rock 'n' roll star, they were the perfect sustenance. Nowadays, you can get a vegan whopper, but you must get rid of the cheese and mayo (which aren't vegan), and that's no fun! Plus, unlike most fast-food burgers, this one gives you the excuse to grill.

YIELD: 2 BURGERS

INGREDIENTS

Burger
- 2 burger buns
- 8 ounces (226 g) plant-based meat (or use a homemade burger, page 30)
- A few drops of liquid smoke (optional)
- 2 slices vegan cheese

Assembly
- Dill pickle slices
- Ketchup
- Onion slices
- Tomato slices
- Iceberg lettuce
- Vegan mayo

INSTRUCTIONS

Burger

1. Toast the buns in a large pan over medium heat, then set them aside. Form the plant-based meat into 2 patties. You can add a very small amount of liquid smoke for that "char-broiled" flavor, if you're going to cook them indoors; this isn't necessary if you're cooking outdoors on a grill.

2. Cook the patties for 3 to 4 minutes per side. If you're cooking them on a grill, I've had the best success by making sure the grill grates are well oiled and cooking them over medium-high heat.

3. No matter how you're cooking them, after flipping the patty, add a slice of vegan cheese. If you're on the grill, close the lid to help melt the cheese. If you're cooking in a pan, add a few drops of water to the pan, then cover to steam and melt the cheese.

Assembly

Once the cheese has melted, assemble the burgers as follows from bottom to top: bottom bun, cheeseburger, pickles, ketchup, onion, tomato, lettuce, vegan mayo, top bun!

ANGRY WHOPPER®

**YIELD: 2 BURGERS
(PLUS EXTRA ONION PETALS AND SAUCE)**

INGREDIENTS

Angry Sauce
- ½ cup (120 g) ketchup
- ¼ cup (60 g) sriracha
- 1 tablespoon (14 g) vegan mayo
- 1 tablespoon (15 ml) pickled jalapeño brine
- 1 teaspoon cayenne pepper

Onion Petals
- 1 large onion
- Neutral oil for frying

Dry batter
- ½ cup (64 g) all-purpose flour
- ½ cup (64 g) cornstarch
- 1 tablespoon (14 g) baking powder
- 2 teaspoons (5 g) smoked paprika
- 2 teaspoons (6 g) chili seasoning
- 2 teaspoons (4 g) garlic powder
- 2 teaspoons (6 g) chipotle powder
- 1 teaspoon salt

Wet batter
- 1 cup (235 ml) unsweetened plant milk, plus more as needed
- 1 tablespoon (15 ml) apple cider vinegar
- 2 tablespoons (28 ml) pickled jalapeño brine
- ¾ cup (94 g) all-purpose flour, plus more as needed

Bread Crumbs
- 1½ cups (170 g) bread crumbs

Burgers
- 2 burger buns
- 8 ounces (226 g) plant-based meat
- Few drops of liquid smoke (optional)
- 2 slices vegan cheese
- 4 slices Rice Paper Bacon (page 28)
- Pickled jalapeños
- Tomato slices
- Iceberg lettuce
- Vegan mayo

INSTRUCTIONS

Angry Sauce

Combine all the ingredients for the Angry Sauce in a small bowl. Refrigerate until needed.

Onion Petals

1. Slice an onion from pole to pole (with the grain, so from root to tip). Let the onions sit in some ice water for 15 minutes.

2. Prepare the dry batter by combining all ingredients in a medium-size bowl. Next, prepare the wet batter by combining all the ingredients in a separate bowl. The batter should be a pancake consistency, so add more flour or liquid as needed. In a third bowl, add the bread crumbs.

3. Heat a 12-inch (30-cm) skillet of neutral oil (e.g., peanut, vegetable, or canola) to 375°F (190°C). Dredge the onions in the flour mixture, then the wet batter, ensuring an even coat and shaking off the excess. Dredge them in the bread crumbs, coating thoroughly.

4. Add the onion petals to the oil carefully. Fry for 2 to 3 minutes, or until a beautiful golden brown. Let them rest on a wire rack. Once all onions are fried up, it's time to make the burgers!

Burgers

1. Toast the buns in a 12-inch (30-cm) pan over medium heat, then set aside. Form the plant-based meat into 2 patties. You can add a very small amount of liquid smoke for that "char-broiled" flavor, if you're going to cook them indoors; this isn't necessary if you're cooking outdoors on a grill.

2. Cook the patties for 3 to 4 minutes per side. If you're cooking them on a grill, I've had the best success by making sure the grill grates are well oiled and cooking them over medium-high heat.

3. No matter how you're cooking them, after flipping the patty, add a slice of vegan cheese. If you're on the grill, close the lid to help melt the cheese. If you're cooking in a pan, add a few drops of water to the pan, then cover to steam and melt the cheese.

Assembly

Once cheese has melted, assemble the burgers as follows from bottom to top: bottom bun, cheeseburger, vegan bacon, pickled jalapeños, angry sauce, onion petals, tomato, lettuce, vegan mayo, top bun!

SHORTCUT

Instead of frying onion petals from scratch, use frozen onion rings or even those fried onions you would use in a green bean casserole!

IN-N-OUT BURGER
DOUBLE-DOUBLE® ANIMAL STYLE®

If the Big Mac was my favorite burger as a kid, this was my favorite as an adult. The lines at this place make it hard to call it fast food, and I often made these at home instead. For the uninitiated, this specific style means adding caramelized onions, pickles, extra sauce, and slathering it all on mustard-grilled patties. Caramelizing onions does take a bit of time, but you'll have plenty of leftovers you can enjoy in a bevy of ways (such as the Whataburger Patty Melt on page 50).

**YIELD: 4 BURGERS
(PLUS EXTRA SAUCE AND ONIONS)**

INGREDIENTS

Sauce

- ▶ 1 cup (225 g) vegan mayo
- ▶ ¼ cup (60 g) ketchup
- ▶ 2 tablespoons (30 g) dill relish
- ▶ 1 tablespoon (15 ml) vegan Worcestershire sauce
- ▶ 1 teaspoon garlic powder
- ▶ Salt and pepper
- ▶ 2 tablespoons (28 g) caramelized onions (optional)

Onions

- ▶ 2 tablespoons (28 ml) neutral oil
- ▶ 2 tablespoons (28 g) vegan butter
- ▶ 3 pound s (1.4 kg) yellow or sweet onions, diced

Burgers

- ▶ 1 pound (454 g) plant-based meat (or use a homemade burger, page 30)
- ▶ 4 hamburger buns
- ▶ Neutral oil or vegan butter for cooking
- ▶ Salt and pepper
- ▶ 3 tablespoons (33 g) yellow mustard
- ▶ 8 slices vegan cheese

Assembly

- ▶ Dill pickle slices
- ▶ Tomato slices
- ▶ Iceberg lettuce

NOTES:

To make Animal Fries, simply top some French fries with plenty of caramelized onions, the burger sauce, and some cheese! Traditionally these are made with a couple slices of American cheese, but I prefer making my Easy Cheese Sauce (page 33)!

CONTINUED

Sauce

Combine everything in a small bowl or plastic container. Store in the fridge until needed.

Onions

1. Add the oil and butter to a large (preferably nonstick skillet) over medium heat. Once the butter is melted and foaming, add the onions and stir to coat them in the butter and oil. Add a healthy pinch of salt and stir to combine.

2. Now the rest of this process is about patience and being attentive! Let the onions sit for 1 to 2 minutes, then stir them around. Continue doing so, until they are a dark brown and taste amazingly sweet and delicious. This may take anywhere from 45 to 70 minutes.

NOTE: Setting a timer for 2 minutes, then stirring and resetting it is a good way to make sure things don't go south. This is a great time to clean up the kitchen or pull up a chair and read a book.

3. If the onions brown too quickly, lower the heat. If they get too dry, add more oil. If they are sticking to the pan, deglaze with 1 tablespoon (15 ml) of water. Just keep an eye on them and adjust your heat accordingly. Once cooked to caramelized perfection, remove them from the pan and set aside.

NOTE: Leftover onions can be stored in the fridge for 1 week. Simply reheat before using. They can also be stored in the freezer. Make sure to use something like an ice cube tray; otherwise they will be a large frozen clump that will be impossible to portion!

Burgers

1. Form eight (2-ounce, or 57-g) patties from the plant-based meat using a burger press or cookie cutter.

2. Bring a 12-inch (30-cm) skillet or griddle up to medium heat with a little oil or vegan butter. Toast the buns. Set them aside and add the burger patties to the pan. Season to taste with salt and pepper. Cook for 3 to 4 minutes, or until browned.

3. Before flipping the patties, squirt about a teaspoon of mustard on them. This might sound strange, but I swear it's amazing! You want just enough to flavor the patty, but don't overdo it or they'll get slippery. Flip the patties, then add a slice of vegan cheese to each patty. Add a little water to the pan, then cover immediately to steam and melt the cheese, about 2–3 minutes.

Assembly

On the bottom bun, slather on some of the sauce, then some dill pickle slices, tomato slice, iceberg lettuce, two cheeseburger patties, plenty of caramelized onions, more sauce, and top bun. ENJOY!

HACKED MENU ITEMS

Hacked or "secret" menu items are some of the best ways to put your own spin on a fast-food order.

At In-N-Out, one of the most popular burgers, the Double-Double Animal Style (page 46), is technically a secret menu item as you won't find it on the actual menu! You can also make some Animal Fries by simply dousing some fries in special sauce, caramelized onions, and cheese. In-N-Out will also make a 3×3 or 4×4, which is a triple or quadruple cheeseburger (see photo on page 46)!

One of my personal favorites used to be a hash brown on my McMuffin (page 120). Back in the day, I would add some ketchup too, but now that I make these at home, I like to spice it up with some sriracha ketchup, (I don't think there's a name yet for that combo!)

A recent fan favorite I clocked is the "McLand, Air, and Sea Burger" which is a behemoth! It's a Big Mac (page 40) combined with a Filet-O-Fish (page 87) and a McChicken Sandwich! I've actually made one and it's oddly delicious. You could totally use the Chick-fil-A recipe (page 58) for the chicken.

What's great about the recipes in this book is you can mash them up yourself in any which way to create your own cross-chain secret menu items. Here are a few ideas based on my own R&D:

- ▶ Combine the biscuits from the Honey Butter Chicken Biscuit (page 126) and McMuffin recipe (page 120) and make a Sausage and Egg Biscuit Sandwich.
- ▶ Combine the McMuffin with the Baconator (page 52) to make a Breakfast Baconator!
- ▶ Pair the waffle from my Waffle House recipe (page 46) with the Chick-fil-A Chick'n and make Chick'n and Waffles.
- ▶ Even though it's not in this book, one of my favorite fast-food burgers of all time is the Western Bacon Cheeseburger from Carl's Jr. Luckily you can make it by using the Onion Rings (page 110), Rice Paper Bacon (page 28), and BBQ Sauce (page 35) right here in this book!

Don't stop there. The desserts are also a playground for your imagination.

- ▶ Try using the vanilla ice cream (page 162) in a root beer float or add it on the side of one of the baked goods like the Apple Pie (page 152).
- ▶ Switch up the fruit used in the Peach Milkshake (page 170) and make yours a strawberry or banana instead. Swirl in some hot fudge from page 164 while you're at it!
- ▶ Double (or triple?) the size of the cinnamon roll on page 155 for a truly monstrous treat.
- ▶ Or get totally wild and use the glazed doughnuts (page 146) as the bun for one of the burgers!

WHATABURGER PATTY MELT

Growing up in California, I never had the opportunity to try out this Texas institution. I know without a doubt if I had grown up in Texas, this place would be my favorite and this burger would be my #1 choice hands down! We are topping these with some caramelized onions and grilling up some Texas toast, but the creamy pepper sauce might be the star of the show. I've had many patty melts in my day, and this one takes the cake!

YIELD: 2 PATTY MELTS (PLUS EXTRA SAUCE AND ONIONS)

INGREDIENTS

Sauce

- ½ cup (115 g) vegan mayo
- 1 teaspoon yellow mustard
- 1 teaspoon vinegar
- 1 tablespoon (16 g) diced chipotles in adobo
- ¼ teaspoon onion powder
- ¼ teaspoon garlic powder
- Salt and pepper

Onions

- 2 tablespoons (28 ml) neutral oil
- 2 tablespoons (28 g) vegan butter
- 3 pounds (1.4 kg) yellow onions, diced

Burgers

- 1 pound (454 g) plant-based meat (or use a homemade burger, page 30)
- Vegan butter, softened
- 4 slices Texas toast
- Salt and pepper
- 4 slices vegan cheese

INSTRUCTIONS

Sauce

Put all the ingredients in blender and blend until smooth.

Onions

Refer to the onion directions for the In-N-Out Double-Double (page 46).

Burgers

1. Form four (4-ounce, or 113-g) patties from the plant-based meat using a burger press or cookie cutter.

2. Spread some softened vegan butter on the Texas toast and add it to a large pan over medium heat. Grill the bread until golden brown, then set aside on a wire rack. Add the burger patties to the pan, and season to taste with salt and pepper. Cook for 3 to 4 minutes, or until browned.

3. Flip the patties, then add a slice of vegan cheese to each patty. Add a little water to the pan, then cover immediately to steam and melt the cheese, about 2–3 minutes.

Assembly

Add both cheeseburger patties to the bottom piece of Texas toast, then a healthy portion of the caramelized onions and creamy pepper sauce. Top with the other piece of Texas toast and ENJOY!

NOTES:

Because this burger is from Texas, it's quite large at 8 ounces (226 g) of meat! Feel free to make it a single patty, it's still super delicious!

If you can't find Texas toast, a good sourdough or rye bread will do just fine, too!

Leftover onions can be used for the Double-Double Animal Style (page 46).

WENDY'S BACONATOR®

You have to love a burger like this, unabashedly upfront about what it is. It's like what if you had a bacon cheeseburger, but it was like the Arnold Schwarzenegger of bacon cheeseburgers! It comes standard with ketchup and mayo, but if you want to eat it the way I used to sub those with either some BBQ Sauce (page 35) or Vegan Ranch (page 35) or both!

YIELD: 2 BURGERS

INGREDIENTS

Burgers

- 12 ounces (340 g) plant-based meat (or use a homemade burger, page 30)
- 2 hamburger buns
- Salt and pepper
- 4 slices vegan cheese

Assembly

- 12 slices Rice Paper Bacon (page 28)
- Vegan mayo
- Ketchup

INSTRUCTIONS

Burgers

1. Form four (3-ounce, or 85-g) square patties from the plant-based meat. This is a bit trickier than the typical round patties. Flatten the meat on some parchment paper, then using a butter knife, press the edges out straight.

2. Heat a large pan over medium heat. Grill the hamburger buns until golden brown, then set them aside. Add the burger patties to the pan, and season to taste with salt and pepper. Cook for 3 to 4 minutes, or until browned.

3. Flip the patties, then add a slice of vegan cheese to each patty. Add a little water to the pan, then cover immediately to steam and melt the cheese, about 2–3 minutes.

Assembly

Add vegan mayo to the bottom bun, then one of the cheeseburger patties. Top with three strips of the vegan bacon, then the other cheeseburger patty. Add three more strips of bacon, then some vegan mayo and ketchup to the top bun. ENJOY!

WHITE CASTLE
THE ORIGINAL SLIDER®

These classic sliders are as easy as they are delicious! I recently visited Las Vegas and tried the Impossible sliders, and I can say with confidence that these are quite similar, if not a little more enjoyable. I learned that they are cooked differently than their regular sliders, which are steamed on a bed of onions, never touching the grill. I tried it both ways with plant-based meat and I didn't like the steaming nearly as much as grilling it directly on the pan. So, I highly encourage that method. (Though of course, feel free to do your own R&D.)

YIELD: 6 SLIDERS

INGREDIENTS

Burgers

▶ 12 ounces (340 g) plant-based meat (or use a homemade burger, page 30)
▶ 6 dinner rolls
▶ 6 slices vegan cheese
▶ 1 large onion, diced

Assembly

▶ Dill pickle slices
▶ Mustard (optional, but recommended)

INSTRUCTIONS

Burgers

1. Line a cutting board with some wax paper or parchment paper. Put the plant-based meat on top, then place another piece of wax paper on top of the meat. Flatten it and roll it into a rectangle shape to match the size of six dinner rolls.

2. Cut the rectangle into two rows of three patties each (for six square patties). Using a bun or roll as a guide for accuracy. Set aside in the fridge.

3. Cut the vegan cheese slices to match the size of the patties. Reserve the cheese scraps for another recipe or meal.

4. In a large skillet over medium heat, grill the onions for 10 to 12 minutes, until translucent and just starting to brown. Remove from the pan and set aside.

5. Toast the slider rolls in the pan until golden brown. Remove and let rest on a wire rack.

6. Add the burger patties to the pan and grill on one side for 3 to 4 minutes, until browned. Then flip, add 1 to 2 tablespoons (15 to 30 g) of the grilled onions on top, followed by a slice of vegan cheese. Add some water to the pan, then cover immediately to melt the cheese for 2–3 minutes.

Assembly

Once the cheese has melted, add the burger patty to the bottom bun. Top with some pickles and a squirt of mustard. ENJOY!

BURGER KING ORIGINAL CHICKEN SANDWICH

This sandwich was something else! It's one of those sandwiches you hate to love. I'm not sure if it was the unnatural shape or what, but I was always simultaneously stoked and afraid to get one. They were overly salty. There was too much mayo on them, and the lettuce was usually weak and wilted. But for some unknown reason, I found myself passing the drive-thru and falling prey to them way too many times!

The good news is, we can make them at home and feel no shame! We can also add as little or as much salt and mayo as we like, and we can use fresh lettuce to boot!

YIELD: 2 SANDWICHES

INGREDIENTS

Chick'n
- 10–12 ounces (283–340 g) vegan chick'n (page 20)
- Neutral oil for frying

Dry Batter
- ¼ cup (32 g) all-purpose flour
- ¼ cup (32 g) cornstarch
- ½ tablespoon (7 g) baking powder
- 1 teaspoon garlic powder
- ½ teaspoon onion powder
- 1–2 teaspoons salt
- ½ teaspoon white pepper
- ½ teaspoon black pepper

Wet Batter
- ½ cup (120 ml) unsweetened plant milk
- ½ tablespoon (8 ml) apple cider vinegar
- 2 tablespoons (16 g) all-purpose flour

Bread Crumbs
- ½ cup (60 g) bread crumbs
- 2 tablespoons (16 g) all-purpose flour
- Salt and pepper

Assembly
- 2 hoagie rolls
- Vegan mayo
- Chopped iceberg lettuce

INSTRUCTIONS

Chick'n

1. I highly recommend using thawed, store-bought vegan chick'n or some tofu because this is such a specifically shaped patty. If you use oyster mushrooms they will still be delicious, but it will be hard to get that long patty shape. So if aesthetics aren't an issue, don't sweat it!

2. Form two chick'n patties that match the length and width of the hoagie rolls. If using store-bought vegan chick'n, place the patties on a parchment-lined baking sheet and throw them in the freezer for 1 hour to firm up.

3. Prepare the dredging stations by combining the ingredients for the batters and the bread crumbs in separate large bowls.

4. Heat a large pot of neutral oil (e.g., peanut, vegetable, or canola) to 375°F (190°C). Once the oil is up to 375°F (190°C), dredge your patties in the dry batter, then the wet batter, and then the bread crumbs. Shake off any excess flour and batter and be sure to get total coverage on each phase.

5. Place the chick'n carefully in the hot oil and let it fry for 4 to 5 minutes, until golden brown. When done, set it aside to rest on a cooling rack. Repeat with the remaining piece of chick'n.

Assembly

Spread some vegan mayo on both sides of the hoagie roll, then add the chick'n and shredded lettuce.

CHICK-FIL-A CHICKEN SANDWICH

Before going vegan, I started making my own Chick-fil-A at home. In fact, that's how I learned to fry chicken in the first place! I soon realized that making these fast-food items at home was infinitely better . . . even when I could easily order from a drive-thru. Maybe it's because I had years of practice. This vegan version is just as good if not better than the classic I remember. The special sauce is one of my favorites! It's good on just about anything, so use leftovers as you wish.

YIELD: 3 SANDWICHES (PLUS EXTRA SAUCE)

INGREDIENTS

Sauce

- ½ cup (115 g) vegan mayo
- ¼ cup (60 ml) BBQ Sauce (page 35)
- 3 tablespoons (33 g) yellow mustard
- 2 tablespoons (40 g) agave or maple syrup
- 1 tablespoon (15 ml) dill pickle brine

Chick'n

- 15 ounces (425 g) vegan chick'n (see page 20)
- Neutral oil for frying

Wet Batter

- 1 cup (235 ml) unsweetened plant milk
- 2 tablespoons (28 ml) hot sauce
- 3 tablespoons (45 ml) dill pickle brine
- 1 tablespoon (15 ml) apple cider vinegar
- ⅓ cup (42 g) all-purpose flour

Dry Batter

- ½ cup (64 g) all-purpose flour
- ½ cup (64 g) cornstarch
- 1 tablespoon (14 g) baking powder
- 1 tablespoon (8 g) Cajun Seasoning (from Cajun Style Fries, page 102)
- 1 teaspoon salt
- Black pepper
- 1–3 tablespoons (5–15 g) cayenne pepper (optional, for a spicy chick'n sandwich)

Assembly

- 3 burger buns
- Dill pickle slices

INSTRUCTIONS

Sauce

Combine all the ingredients in a small bowl or plastic container. Refrigerate until needed.

Chick'n

1. Form three (5-ounce, or 142 g) chick'n patties from the vegan chick'n the same size as the burger buns. If using thawed store-bought vegan chick'n, add the patties to a parchment-lined baking sheet and throw in the freezer for 1 hour to firm up.

2. Prepare the dredging stations by combining the ingredients for each batter in their own bowls.

3. Heat a large pot of neutral oil (e.g., peanut, vegetable, or canola) to 375°F (190°C).

4. Once the oil is up to 375°F (190°C), dredge your patties in the dry batter, then the wet batter, and then back into the dry batter. Shake off any excess flour and batter and be sure to get total coverage on each phase.

5. Place a chick'n piece carefully in the hot oil and let it fry for 4 to 5 minutes, until golden brown. Let it rest on a cooling rack and repeat with the remaining two pieces of chick'n.

Assembly

Toast the buns in a pan over medium heat. Add some of the sauce to the bottom bun, followed by some pickles, the vegan chick'n, more sauce and top bun. Enjoy!

WHATABURGER BUFFALO RANCH STRIP CHICKEN SANDWICH

I think it's weird that we don't see more sandwiches comprised of chicken tenders. You get more surface area of the crunchy, tasty bits—just like with a double or triple cheeseburger. And this sandwich is as crunchy and tasty as they get! There's a debate about whether ranch or bleu cheese is the best when paired with buffalo sauce. That case may be closed once you make one of these! To make another classic sandwich, swap the buns for Texas toast and instead of using buffalo and ranch, use some BBQ Sauce (page 35) to make a BBQ Chick'n Strip Sandwich!

YIELD: 3 SANDWICHES

INGREDIENTS

Chick'n

▶ 15 ounces (425 g) vegan chick'n (see page 20)

▶ Neutral oil for frying

Dry Batter

▶ ½ cup (64 g) all-purpose flour

▶ ½ cup (64 g) cornstarch

▶ 1 tablespoon (14 g) baking powder

▶ 1 teaspoon salt

▶ 1 teaspoon garlic powder

▶ 2 teaspoons (5 g) smoked paprika

▶ 2 teaspoons (4 g) onion powder

▶ 1 teaspoon mushroom seasoning or more salt

▶ ½ teaspoon ground sage

▶ ½ teaspoon ground coriander

▶ ½ teaspoon chipotle powder

▶ Black pepper

Wet Batter

▶ 1 cup (235 ml) unsweetened plant milk

▶ 1 tablespoon (15 ml) apple cider vinegar

▶ 1 tablespoon (15 ml) hot sauce

▶ ⅓ cup (42 g) all-purpose flour

Assembly

▶ 3 large burger buns

▶ 6 slices vegan cheese

▶ Vegan ranch, store-bought or homemade (page 35)

▶ A few tablespoons Frank's RedHot® Buffalo Wings Hot Sauce

INSTRUCTIONS

Chick'n

1. Form nine (2-ounce, or 57-g) chick'n strips from the vegan chick'n. If using thawed store-bought vegan chick'n, add the strips to a parchment-lined baking sheet and throw in the freezer for 1 hour to firm up.

2. Prepare the dredging stations by combining the ingredients for each batter in separate bowls.

3. Heat a large pot of neutral oil (e.g., peanut, vegetable, or canola) to 375°F (190°C).

4. Once the oil is up to 375°F (190°C), dredge the chick'n strips in the dry batter, then the wet batter, and then back into the dry batter. Shake off any excess flour and batter and be sure to get total coverage on each phase.

5. You can fry three to four pieces at a time, as long as you don't crowd the pot. Place the pieces carefully in the hot oil and let it fry for 4 to 5 minutes, until golden brown. Let the strips rest on a cooling rack and repeat with the remaining pieces.

Assembly

1. Add the buns to a large, lightly oiled pan over medium heat. Toast them until golden brown. Once toasted, flip the buns over and lower the heat. Add a slice of vegan cheese to each bun and cover to melt. It might take a little while, but it's worth it! A kitchen torch will also melt the cheese nicely if you have one.

2. Once the cheese is melted, make the sandwiches by adding three chick'n strips to one bun. Top with plenty of vegan ranch and buffalo sauce, then add the top bun and enjoy!

KFC NASHVILLE HOT CHICKEN SANDWICH

So, the Nashville Hot Chicken was the last piece of non-vegan chicken I ever ate. I remember it was super greasy and made me feel horrible for about six hours after. I can confidently say that this recipe is a cut above, and I felt great after eating it! No lingering "meat sweats" or anything. In fact, this might be my favorite fried chick'n recipe in this book.

YIELD: 3 SANDWICHES

INGREDIENTS

Chick'n
- 15 ounces (425 g) vegan chick'n (see page 20)
- Neutral oil for frying

Secret Seasoning
- 2 teaspoons (12 g) salt
- ½ tablespoon (2 g) dried thyme
- ½ tablespoon (3 g) dried basil
- 1 teaspoon dried oregano
- 1 tablespoon (12 g) celery salt
- 1 tablespoon (6 g) black pepper
- 3 tablespoons (18 g) white pepper
- 1 tablespoon (11 g) mustard powder

- ¼ cup (28 g) paprika
- 2 tablespoons (30 g) garlic salt
- 1 tablespoon (6 g) ground ginger

Dry Batter
- ½ cup (64 g) all-purpose flour
- ½ cup (64 g) cornstarch
- 1 tablespoon (14 g) baking powder
- 6 tablespoons (52 g) Secret Seasoning

Wet Batter
- 1 cup (235 ml) unsweetened plant milk
- 1 tablespoon (15 ml) apple cider vinegar

- ¼ cup (60 ml) hot sauce
- ⅓ cup (42 g) all-purpose flour

Nashville Style Hot Sauce
- 3 tablespoons (15 g) cayenne pepper
- ½ tablespoon (8 g) packed brown sugar
- 1 teaspoon garlic salt
- 1 teaspoon black pepper
- ½–1 cup (118–236 ml) oil from frying

Assembly
- 3 burger buns
- Vegan mayo
- Dill pickle slic

INSTRUCTIONS

Chick'n

1. Form three (5-ounce, or 142-g) chick'n patties from the vegan chick'n the same size as the burger buns. Refrigerate until needed.

2. Combine the Secret Seasoning ingredients in a small bowl.

3. Combine the ingredients for each batter in separate bowls.

4. Heat a large pot of neutral oil (e.g., peanut, vegetable, or canola) to 375°F (190°C).

5. Dredge the patties in the dry batter, then the wet batter, and then back into the dry batter. Shake off any excess flour and batter and be sure to get total coverage on each phase.

6. Place the patties in the hot oil and fry for 4 to 5 minutes, until golden brown. Let them rest on a cooling rack for 30

seconds. Using a ladle, carefully scoop out about ½ to 1 cup (120 to 235 ml) of the cooking oil. Add it to a bowl with the Nashville style hot sauce dry ingredients. Whisk it to incorporate, then dunk your fried chick'n patties and carefully toss them in the oil (one at a time is advised).

NOTE: It is crucial that the chick'n and the Nashville hot sauce both be hot when applying. This will prevent the chick'n from getting soggy!

Assembly

Toast the buns in a large pan over medium heat. Add some vegan mayo to the bottom bun, followed by some pickles, the Nashville hot chick'n, more mayo, and the top bun. Enjoy!

FAST-FOOD FOOD

FAVORITES

CHAPTER 3

TACO BELL CRUNCHWRAP SUPREME®

TACO BELL CHEESY GORDITA CRUNCH

TACO BELL MEXICAN PIZZA

DOMINO'S PAN PIZZA

PANERA WHITE CHEDDAR MAC 'N' CHEESE

MCDONALD'S MCRIB®

SUBWAY'S MEATBALL SUB

CHIPOTLE BURRITO BOWL

MCDONALD'S FILET-O-FISH®

PANDA EXPRESS KUNG PAO CHICKEN

TACO BELL CRUNCHWRAP SUPREME®

One of the most iconic fast-food items of the past thirty years, this has been a favorite of mine for a while now. I would even argue that this is the best way to eat a burrito as you are guaranteed a little of everything in each bite! As a vegan, I can easily order one and customize it however I want: sub beef with beans, fresco style, add guacamole, potatoes, and jalapeños. However, making these at home with vegan beef, cheese, and sour cream as the original is constructed is vastly superior. And I say that as somebody who loves refried beans and potatoes with every fiber of my being!

YIELD: 4 SERVINGS

INGREDIENTS

Beef

▶ Neutral oil for cooking

▶ 1 pound (454 g) plant-based meat or TVP Ground Beef (page 30)

▶ 3 tablespoons (21 g) Taco Seasoning (page 37)

▶ Salt and pepper

▶ 1 cup (235 ml) water

▶ 1 tablespoon (15 ml) lime juice

Assembly

▶ 4 large flour tortillas

▶ 1 cup (235 ml) Easy Cheese Sauce (page 33)

▶ 4 tostadas

▶ ½ cup (115 g) vegan sour cream, store-bought or homemade (page 86)

▶ 2 cups (110 g) shredded iceberg lettuce

▶ 1 large tomato, diced

▶ Neutral oil for cooking

INSTRUCTIONS

Beef

1. Add 1 tablespoon (15 ml) of neutral oil to a large skillet and heat up over medium heat. Add the plant-based meat and crumble. Cook for 4 to 5 minutes, or until the beef starts to brown. Add all the spices. Stir to combine.

2. Add the water and lime juice. Stir to combine, then reduce until there's just a little bit of liquid left.

SHORTCUTS

You can use store-bought taco seasoning to taste for the beef. While this will be quicker, you won't achieve the next-level depth of flavor of this recipe!

You can also use shredded vegan cheese instead of the cheese sauce, but it won't be as decadent.

Assembly

1. Heat up the tortillas in a microwave for 30 seconds. Place one-quarter of the beef mixture in the middle of each one. Then, top with ¼ cup (60 ml) of the cheese sauce. Add the tostada, spread about 2 tablespoons (28 g) of vegan sour cream on top. Then, add the shredded lettuce and diced tomato.

2. To wrap them up, fold over the bottom half of the tortilla, then continue counterclockwise folding over the rest of the tortilla to create pleats. If the tortilla isn't big enough to cover the filling, simply cut out a section from another tortilla to patch it up.

3. Bring a pan up to medium heat with a little oil. Turn the wrap over so the pleated side hits the pan. This will help ensure that it doesn't become unwrapped. Grill for 2 to 3 minutes, or until golden brown. Flip and grill the other side for 2 to 3 minutes, until browned.

TACO BELL CHEESY GORDITA CRUNCH

As I mentioned in the previous recipe, this fast-food stop is great about allowing substitutions to make items vegetarian or vegan friendly. That said, I think there's no way to enjoy a gordita to the max without that signature cheese. So naturally, when I started making vegan fast food at home, this was high on the list.

YIELD: 4 SERVINGS

INGREDIENTS

Spicy Ranch

- 1 cup (235 ml) vegan ranch, store-bought or homemade (page 35)
- ½ teaspoon cayenne pepper
- ½ teaspoon chipotle powder

Beef

- Neutral oil for cooking
- 12 ounces (340 g) plant-based meat or TVP Ground Beef (page 30)
- 2 tablespoons (14 g) Taco Seasoning (page 37)
- Salt and pepper
- ¾ cup (175 ml) water or beefless broth
- Juice of 1 lime

Assembly

- 4 flatbreads
- 1 cup (235 g) Easy Cheese Sauce (page 33)
- 4 hard taco shells
- 2 cups (110 g) shredded iceberg lettuce
- 1 cup (115 g) shredded vegan cheese

INSTRUCTIONS

Spicy Ranch

Simply combine the ranch and spices in a small bowl, adding more for more heat! Store in the refrigerator until needed.

Beef

1. Add 1 tablespoon (15 ml) of neutral oil to a large skillet and heat up over medium heat. Add the plant-based meat and crumble. Cook for 4 to 5 minutes, or until the beef starts to brown. Next, add all the spices. Stir to combine.

2. Add the water and lime juice. Stir to combine, then reduce until there's just a little bit of liquid left.

Assembly

1. Heat up the flatbreads in a microwave or over a burner on the stove for 30 seconds. Slather on plenty of the vegan cheese sauce. Gently place the hard-shell taco inside and fold the flatbread around it. The cheese sauce will bind them together like two people hugging.

2. Add one-quarter of the beef mixture in the middle of each one. Top with a good drizzle of the spicy ranch, ½ cup (28 g) of the shredded lettuce, and ¼ cup (30 g) of the shredded vegan cheese. Dig in immediately!

TACO BELL MEXICAN PIZZA

If you've ever ordered this classic, then you know this dish is neither authentic Mexican food, nor pizza . . . but that really doesn't matter. After one bite, you'll agree this recipe is nothing short of a masterpiece!

YIELD: 4 MEXICAN PIZZAS

INGREDIENTS

Beef

- Neutral oil for cooking
- 1 pound (454 g) plant-based meat or TVP Ground Beef (page 30)
- ¼ cup (30 g) pickled jalapeños, chopped
- 3 tablespoons (21 g) Taco Seasoning (page 37)
- Salt and pepper
- 1 cup (235 ml) water
- 1 tablespoon (15 ml) lime juice

Beans

- 2 cans (15 ounces, or 425 g each) pinto beans
- ¼–½ cup (60–120 ml) unsweetened plant milk
- 3 tablespoons (21 g) Taco Seasoning (page 37)
- 2 tablespoons (28 ml) lime juice
- 2 tablespoons (32 g) diced chipotles in adobo
- Salt and pepper

Red Sauce

- 2 tablespoons (28 g) vegan butter or neutral oil
- 2 tablespoons (16 g) all-purpose flour
- 1 cup (235 ml) vegetable stock
- 1 can (8 ounces, or 226 g) tomato sauce
- 2 tablespoons (28 ml) pickled jalapeño brine
- 2 tablespoons (32 g) diced chipotles in adobo
- 1 tablespoon (15 ml) lime juice
- 2 tablespoons (14 g) Taco Seasoning (page 37)
- Dash of ground cinnamon
- Salt and pepper

Assembly

- Neutral oil for cooking
- 8 flour tortillas (large soft taco size)
- 8 ounces (226 g) shredded vegan cheese or American Cheese Hack (page 33)
- 1 large tomato, diced
- Toppings of your choice, such as chopped fresh chives or green onions, black olives, and shredded iceberg lettuce

NOTE:

I like using some of the liquid the beans are packaged in for refried beans. If you don't, simply wash them and adjust the plant milk levels to the consistency of your choice!

CONTINUED

Beef

1. Add 1 tablespoon (15 ml) of neutral oil to a large skillet over medium heat. Add the plant-based meat and crumble. Cook for 4 to 5 minutes, or until the beef starts to brown. Next, add the jalapeños and all the spices. Stir to combine.

2. Add the water and lime juice. Stir to combine, then reduce until there's just a little bit of liquid left.

Beans

Drain and wash the beans (or reserve the liquid). Add them to a large saucepan over medium heat. Add ¼ cup (60 ml) of the plant milk. Mash to your desired consistency. If they are too dry, add more plant milk. Add the spices, lime juice, chipotles in adobo, salt, and pepper and stir to incorporate. Taste and adjust the seasonings. Keep warm on low heat.

Red Sauce

1. Heat up the vegan butter in a saucepan over medium heat. Once melted, add 1 tablespoon (8 g) of the flour, and whisk to combine. Repeat with the rest of the flour.

2. Slowly add the vegetable stock, whisking the entire time. Once the veggie stock is whisked in, add everything else and stir to combine. Taste and adjust for seasoning, then reduce for 8 to 10 minutes, or until the consistency is like a thick pizza sauce. Cover and keep warm over low heat.

Tortillas & Assembly

1. Add a layer of neutral oil to a wide skillet and heat to around 350°F (175°C or gas mark 4). Fry one tortilla at a time until crispy and golden brown. Let them rest on a wire rack.

2. For each pizza: Lay down one fried tortilla on a baking sheet, top with beans, then the ground beef. Add another fried tortilla and spread a nice layer of the red sauce over it. Top with 2 ounces (57 g) of the shredded cheese.

3. Place the pizzas in the oven under the broiler and set to high. This will melt the cheese but keep an eye on it to avoid burning the tortilla. Once all the cheese has melted, top with the diced tomatoes and any other toppings you prefer.

SHORTCUTS

To save time, use canned refried beans and premade red enchilada sauce.

You can also use store-bought taco seasoning to taste for the beef and beans. While this will be quicker, you won't achieve the next-level depth of flavor of this recipe!

DOMINO'S PAN PIZZA

Like most Americans, I grew up eating a ton of pizza. I know a lot of folks like a bunch of toppings, but for my money, I liked pepperoni (and maybe throw on some jalapeños and pineapple!). No matter your preference, this recipe will get you a solid base, as we'll focus on the mozzarella. Cheese is the main star of pizza, and in my experience, the thing that can make or break a vegan pizza. This cheese is so far my favorite, and it avoids the common pitfalls of vegan cheese, namely, the gloopy texture. To make this even easier—and more delicious if you ask me—we'll be making this in a cast-iron skillet for a pan pizza as well!

YIELD: 1 PIZZA

NOTE: There will be enough dough and cheese for two pizzas with this recipe. To make two pizzas, just double the sauce. The vegan mozzarella can go to use elsewhere! If you freeze leftover dough, thaw it in the fridge and let it come to room temperature before using.

CONTINUED

INGREDIENTS

Mozzarella Cheese
(Makes enough for 3 to 4 pizzas)

- ▶ ¼ cup (34 g) raw cashews
- ▶ Boiling water for soaking
- ▶ 2 teaspoons (5 g) psyllium husk powder plus ¼ cup (60 ml) water
- ▶ 1½ cups (355 ml) unsweetened plant milk
- ▶ ¼ cup (54 g) refined coconut oil, melted
- ▶ 1½ teaspoons lactic acid
- ▶ 1 teaspoon salt, or more to taste
- ▶ 2 tablespoons (15 g) tapioca starch
- ▶ 1½ tablespoons (15 g) kappa carrageenan

Pizza Dough
(Makes enough for 2 pizzas)

- ▶ 4 cups (480 g) bread flour, plus more if needed
- ▶ 2¼ teaspoons (7 g) instant yeast
- ▶ 2 tablespoons (26 g) sugar
- ▶ 2 teaspoons (12 g) salt
- ▶ 1½ cups (355 ml) warm water, heated to 110°F (43°C)
- ▶ 2 tablespoons (28 ml) olive oil, plus more for coating the bowl

Pizza

- ▶ ¼–⅓ cup (60–80 ml) pizza sauce
- ▶ Vegan pepperoni or any desired toppings
- ▶ Olive oil
- ▶ Salt
- ▶ Nutritional yeast
- ▶ Cornmeal
- ▶ Cooking oil spray

> **NOTE:** Agar agar powder can be used instead of kappa carrageenan. Agar agar will result in a stretchier cheese; however, I prefer the consistency of cheese made with the kappa carrageenan.

INSTRUCTIONS

RECIPE CROSSOVER

Use the extra mozzarella in another pizza or the Mozzarella Sticks (page 112).

Mozzarella Cheese

1. Cover the cashews in boiling water for 10 minutes, then drain. Combine the psyllium husk powder and cool water in a cup for 5 minutes, until thickened.

2. This part is important: Once this process starts, it cannot stop. Make sure to have everything set up for speed and efficiency.

3. Have a silicone or glass container ready next to the blender. Heat the plant milk until just boiling. Quickly but carefully add the hot plant milk to the blender. Add everything EXCEPT the tapioca starch and kappa carrageenan. Blend on high speed until smooth, quickly (and carefully!) taste and adjust for seasoning.

4. While the blender is still going, add the tapioca starch followed by the kappa carrageenan. This is where SCIENCE happens. Once the kappa reacts to the heat in the plant milk it will begin to solidify. If the blender starts to sound like it's having a hard time, that's a good sign that it's setting, and it's time to quickly transfer the cheese to a silicone mold or glass container. Refrigerate it for at least 4 hours. After that, it should be firm enough to grate. If not, pop it in the freezer for 15 to 20 minutes.

Dough

1. In the bowl of a stand mixer, combine the bread flour, instant yeast, sugar, and salt. Using the dough hook, turn the stand mixer on low speed and add the water and oil. Once the wet and dry ingredients have combined, turn the speed up to medium and let it mix for 5 to 7 minutes. The dough should be tacky but not too sticky. If it's sticking to the side of the bowl, add 1 tablespoon (8 g) of flour at a time until it pulls away and forms a dough ball.

2. Lightly grease a large bowl. Add the dough ball, and cover with a kitchen towel or plastic wrap. Let the dough rise for 1 to 2 hours, or until doubled in size.

Pizza

1. Preheat the oven to 550°F (288°C), or as high as it will go if it can't get up there. Dump the dough onto a floured surface and knead it for a minute into a ball. Cut it in half, each piece should weigh about 15 ounces (420 g). Stretch one into a circle about the size of a 12-inch (30-cm) cast-iron pan. Speaking of which, get a 12-inch (30-cm) cast-iron pan and grease it with 2 tablespoons (28 ml) of oil, sprinkle it with some salt and nutritional yeast, as well as a little cornmeal and spread them out evenly.

2. Lay down the dough and stretch it out so it fits snuggly in the cast-iron pan. Form a crust around the edge if desired. Spread the pizza sauce evenly, ¼ cup (60 ml) should be enough: Add a little more if desired, but not too much, otherwise the pizza will be too dang wet! Grate 1 cup (115 g) of the vegan mozzarella and spread it evenly over the pizza. Add the pepperoni or any toppings desired, and then lightly spray the top with cooking oil, this helps the cheese melt even better!

3. Pop the pizza in the oven for 10 to 12 minutes, or until the cheese is melted and bubbling. Broil on high for 2 minutes to get a bit of browning (optional). Remove the pizza from the oven, let it cool for 5 to 10 minutes, then slice and serve!

PANERA WHITE CHEDDAR MAC 'N' CHEESE

I rarely went to Panera before going vegan, but this was easily the dish I ordered the most! I mean, it's mac 'n' cheese plus white cheddar? How could you not?! This white cheddar sauce is cashew based, so you might think it would be too mild. But wait, there's a secret ingredient: That's right, the lactic acid will impart that signature TANG! If cashews aren't your thing, fret not, there's an option to make it with the easy cheese sauce as well! Both are equally delicious!

YIELD: 4 SERVINGS

INGREDIENTS

Pasta

- 8 ounces (226 g) pipe rigate or elbow macaroni
- Freshly cracked black pepper

White Cheddar Cheese Sauce

- 1 cup (137 g) raw cashews
- Boiling water for soaking
- 2 cups (475 ml) unsweetened plant milk
- 2 tablespoons (10 g) nutritional yeast
- 2 teaspoons (6 g) lactic acid
- 1 teaspoon garlic powder
- 1 teaspoon salt
- ½ teaspoon onion powder
- 1 tablespoon (8 g) mushroom seasoning

Easy Sauce (White Cheddar)

- 4 ounces (120 ml) water
- ½ teaspoon sodium citrate
- 8 ounces (226 g) shredded vegan mozzarella cheese
- 2 teaspoons (6 g) lactic acid
- 1 teaspoon garlic powder
- ½ teaspoon onion powder
- 1 teaspoon salt
- 1 tablespoon (8 g) mushroom seasoning
- 1 tablespoon (8 g) tapioca starch

INSTRUCTIONS

Pasta

Cook the pasta according to the package instructions.

White Cheddar Sauce

While the pasta is cooking, soak the cashews in boiling water for 15 minutes to soften them. Drain the cashews. Add all the ingredients to a high-speed blender and blend until smooth.

Easy Sauce

Add the water to a medium saucepan and bring to a boil. Add the sodium citrate and stir to dissolve. Add the vegan cheese, seasonings, and tapioca starch. Whisk until melted and smooth.

NOTE: Instead of sodium citrate, whisk in unsweetened plant milk in ¼-cup (60-ml) increments until the cheese sauce is smooth and velvety.

Assembly

Taste the sauce and adjust for seasoning, then pour it over the cooked pasta. Serve with freshly cracked black pepper and enjoy!

MCDONALD'S MCRIB®

To be honest, I never understood the hype with this sandwich. On paper it looks great; I mean anything drenched in BBQ sauce and covered in pickles and onions is sure to be a winner. But every time I tried one, I was ultimately disappointed. That may put me in the minority, but it encouraged me to make the vegan version better than the original. (I think I succeeded, but you'll have to be the judge of how much you like my BBQ Sauce.) For this recipe, you have two options: a homemade seitan jackfruit version and a shortcut using some store-bought plant-based meat. I like both, but for convenience it's hard to beat the shortcut.

YIELD: 6 SANDWICHES

INGREDIENTS

Seitan Jackfruit
- 1 can (14 oz, or 397 g) jackfruit, drained
- Neutral oil for preparing the pan

Dry Mixture
- ¾ cup (84 g) vital wheat gluten, plus more if needed
- ¼ cup (24 g) chickpea flour
- 1 tablespoon (7 g) smoked paprika
- 1 tablespoon (7 g) garlic powder
- 1 tablespoon (8 g) chili seasoning
- 1 teaspoon ground cumin
- 2 tablespoons (10 g) nutritional yeast

Wet Mixture
(Makes 2 cups [475 ml], use half for braising)
- 1 tablespoon (8 g) mushroom seasoning
- 2 tablespoons (28 ml) soy sauce
- 2 tablespoons (40 g) agave or maple syrup
- 1 tablespoon (15 g) sriracha
- 1½ cups (355 ml) beefless broth
- 2 tablespoons (32 g) tomato paste
- 1 tablespoon (15 ml) neutral oil
- 1 teaspoon liquid smoke
- 1 teaspoon onion powder

Assembly
- 2–3 cups (475–705 ml) BBQ Sauce (page 35)
- 6 hoagie rolls, toasted
- Dill pickle slices
- 1 cup (115 g) sliced onions

INSTRUCTIONS

Seitan Jackfruit

1. Drain the jackfruit and steam in a steamer basket for 12 minutes. While the jackfruit is steaming, combine all the ingredients for the dry mixture in one large bowl, and all the ingredients for the wet mixture in a second large bowl.

2. Preheat the oven to 350°F (175°C or gas mark 4), and lightly grease a baking pan. Once the jackfruit is steamed, mash it with a potato masher until it is finely shredded, removing the seeds if necessary. Combine the shredded jackfruit with the dry mixture. Then add half of the wet mixture (about 1 cup [235 ml]).

CONTINUED

3. Stir the seitan mix first with a wood spoon, then knead it in the bowl by hand. This type of seitan will be looser and wetter than typical seitan, but if it's so wet it won't stick together, add a tablespoon of vital wheat gluten at a time and knead in until it forms a ball.

4. Knead the seitan dough on a cutting board lined with wax paper or parchment paper for 2 minutes, until the dough feels like a cohesive ball. Flatten the dough to 1½ inches (3.5 cm) and divide into six equal portions, about 3½ ounces (100 g) each.

5. Shape the patties (use a hoagie roll as a guide). Add patties to the prepared baking pan. Cover them in the rest of the wet mixture to braise

6. Bake at 350°F (175°C or gas mark 4) for 50 minutes, flipping halfway through. If after the first 25 minutes the braising liquid has mostly evaporated, add some water so the patties don't dry out. The patties will still be delicate so flip and handle with care! Check the liquid level every so often to make sure they don't dry out. Add a little water, if needed.

7. Once the patties are cooked through, heat up a 12-inch (30-cm) skillet with a bit of oil. Brush and coat the patties with BBQ sauce. Grill for 2 to 3 minutes, flip them and brush with more sauce. Grill for 2 to 3 minutes. Some charring is not only natural but encouraged! That's flavor!

Assembly

Once the patties have been grilled on both sides, brush them with some more BBQ sauce. Add them to a toasted hoagie roll with pickles, onions, and more sauce if desired. DIG IN!!

SHORTCUTS

You can use plant-based meat instead of seitan as a shortcut! Simply mix the steamed jackfruit with 24 ounces (680 g) of plant-based meat (no need to make either the wet or dry mixtures). Form your patties, season with a dry BBQ rub, and grill them on a pan over medium heat until browned on both sides. Then brush with BBQ sauce and grill for 2 minutes on each side to caramelize the BBQ sauce. Serve on a hoagie roll with pickles, onions, and more BBQ sauce if desired. It's great on the BBQ grill too!

SUBWAY MEATBALL SUB

You can tell a lot about someone by their favorite sub sandwich. I can say, without any guilt, that this meatball sub is the one I ordered most in my teens and twenties! To replicate this iconic sandwich in the best way possible, just follow the recipe. But feel free to riff on it as well: Use your favorite jarred sauce instead of making it from scratch or experiment with adding cheese (sliced, untoasted for fidelity; or a sprinkle of vegan parmesan for a boost of umami).

YIELD: 4 TO 5 SANDWICHES (DEPENDING ON HOW FULL YOU STUFF THEM)

CONTINUED

INGREDIENTS

Meatballs

- 1 pound (454 g) plant-based meat
- ½ cup (64 g) finely diced onion
- 4 cloves garlic, minced
- 2 tablespoons (10 g) grated vegan parmesan
- 2 tablespoons (8 g) chopped fresh parsley
- 1 teaspoon dried oregano
- 1 teaspoon red pepper flakes
- 3 tablespoons (45 ml) unsweetened plant milk
- ⅓ cup (38 g) bread crumbs
- Olive oil for cooking

Marinara Sauce

- 2 tablespoons (28 ml) olive oil
- 4 cloves garlic, minced
- 1 can (28 ounces, or 794 g) San Marzano tomatoes, crushed
- 1 teaspoon red pepper flakes
- 2 teaspoons (2 g) dried oregano
- Salt and pepper

Cheese Sauce

- ½ batch Easy Cheese Sauce (page 33; use vegan mozzarella instead of cheddar)

Assembly

- 4–5 hoagie rolls

INSTRUCTIONS

Meatballs

1. In a large bowl, mix all the ingredients for the meatballs. Using a small scooper, scoop out about 1 ounce (28 g) of meat and then roll by hand into a meatball.

2. Heat up 1 tablespoon (15 ml) of olive oil in a large skillet over medium heat. Add the meatballs and cook for 3 minutes undisturbed, until one side is nicely browned. Turn them over on to the other side and cook for 3 minutes. Brown as many sides as desired, then remove the meatballs from the pan and set aside.

Marinara Sauce

1. In the same pan, make the marinara sauce. Add the olive oil and heat up for 1 minute. Add the garlic and cook for 1 to 2 minutes, being careful not to burn it. Once it's lightly toasted, add the tomatoes, red pepper flakes, oregano, and salt and pepper to taste. Stir to combine everything and then bring to a light boil. Lower the heat to simmer for 15 to 20 minutes, or until reduced to the desired consistency. Taste and adjust for seasoning.

2. Add the meatballs back in and let them simmer for 6 minutes, or until cooked through. Cover and keep warm over low heat.

Cheese Sauce

Prepare a half-batch of Easy Cheese Sauce (page 33) with vegan mozzarella instead of cheddar.

NOTE: If you want to go ahead and serve it up as is, that would be closer to the original. But I highly recommend making a quick garlic bread with your hoagie rolls. Simply combine ½ cup (112 g) softened vegan butter with 4 cloves of minced garlic and 1 tablespoon (4 g) of chopped fresh parsley. Spread 2 tablespoons (28 g) of that mixture on each hoagie roll. Place them on a baking sheet and broil them for 4 to 5 minutes, until golden brown and toasted. You can also panfry them if you prefer.

Assembly

Take four to five meatballs and place them in each hoagie roll. Add a couple more tablespoons of the marinara, and as much cheese sauce as desired!

CHIPOTLE BURRITO BOWL

This is one of those places that I was super stoked about when I first started going, and for fast food, they have a decent number of vegan options. However, the more I went there, the less exciting I found it. In fact, in doing research for this book, I tried a bowl for the first time in years, and I found it to be a little disappointing. Hence, this recipe, which I think you'll find is reminiscent of the original, only way more flavorful and vibrant! Add toppings such as grilled bell peppers, pico de gallo, roasted corn salsa, or go off the typical topping bar and add black olives or pickled jalapeños, whatever you like!

YIELD: 3 TO 4 SERVINGS

INGREDIENTS

Chick'n

- 1 tablespoon (8 g) mushroom seasoning
- 1 teaspoon ground coriander
- 1 teaspoon ground cumin
- ¼ teaspoon ground cinnamon
- 3 tablespoons (48 g) chipotles in adobo
- 3 cloves garlic, peeled
- Juice of ½ lime
- ½ cup (120 ml) vegetable stock
- Salt
- 8 ounces (226 g) vegan chick'n (page 20), chopped into bite-sized pieces

Beans

- 2 cans (15 ounces, or 425 g each) black beans, drained
- 1 jalapeño, diced (optional)
- 1 tablespoon (7 g) Taco Seasoning (page 37)
- Juice of ½ lime
- Salt

Rice

- 4 cups (660 g) cooked rice
- Juice of 1 lime
- ⅓ cup (5 g) chopped fresh cilantro
- 2 tablespoons (28 g) vegan butter
- 2 cloves garlic, minced
- Salt

Assembly

- 1 avocado, cubed
- 1 cup (256 g) pico de gallo
- 1 cup (160 g) roasted corn
- ½ cup (115 g) vegan sour cream, store-bought or homemade (page 86)
- Hot sauce

INSTRUCTIONS

Chick'n

1. Add everything but the vegan chick'n to a blender and blend until smooth. Taste and adjust for seasoning. It should be smoky, savory, and delicious!

2. In a large skillet over medium heat, cook the vegan chick'n until slightly browned, then add the sauce. Cook for 5 minutes, or until the chick'n is cooked through and the sauce is fragrant and slightly thickened.

Beans

Add everything to a pot and stir to combine. Leave out the jalapeño for less spicy beans. This comes together super quickly: Stir and cook until heated through. Taste and adjust for seasoning, but these should be super good and zippy!

CONTINUED

INSTRUCTIONS

Rice

Mix the rice ingredients together in a medium bowl. The vegan butter should melt and coat the rice thoroughly. Taste and adjust for seasoning as always!

Assembly

Assemble by adding about 1 cup (165 to 220 g) of rice to a bowl, followed by the black beans and the chick'n. Top with avocado, pico de gallo, roasted corn, vegan sour cream, or hot sauce!

SOUR CREAM

In addition to the rice, many people love the "sour cream" at Chipotle, which is quite a bit thinner and more citrusy than store-bought sour cream. If you'd like to add some to your bowl, give this a try.

- ▶ 1 cup (137 g) raw cashews
- ▶ ⅓ cup (80 ml) full-fat coconut milk
- ▶ 1–2 teaspoons (3–6 g) lactic acid, or more to taste
- ▶ ½–1 teaspoon salt, or more to taste
- ▶ ½ cup (120 ml) unsweetened plant milk (use more for a thinner sour cream)
- ▶ 1 tablespoon (15 ml) lime juice, or more to taste
- ▶ ⅛ teaspoon xanthan gum (optional)

Soak the cashews in boiling hot water for 10 to 15 minutes. Add everything except the xanthan gum to a high-speed blender and blend until smooth. If using the xanthan gum to thicken your sour cream, add it now with the blender running. Taste and adjust for seasoning . . . very important!

MCDONALD'S FILET-O-FISH®

Talk about an ultimate love it or hate it menu item! While I was never a fan, I could see it being craveable for vegans who used to enjoy fried fish. I will admit this sandwich deviates in a couple ways from the classic. First, the fish substitute is probably a bit more flavorful (and in 9 out of 10 cases, crispier!). I also use an entire slice of cheese, whereas the original only uses a half slice for some bizarre reason. Oh, and I have a feeling if I ordered this today, I would add pickles to it, so feel free to do that as well!

**YIELD: 3 SANDWICHES
(PLUS EXTRA SAUCE)**

CONTINUED

INGREDIENTS

Tartar Sauce
- 1 cup (225 g) vegan mayo
- 2 tablespoons (30 g) dill relish
- 1 tablespoon (9 g) chopped capers
- 1 tablespoon (15 ml) lemon juice
- 1 tablespoon (4 g) chopped fresh dill
- 2 cloves garlic, minced
- Salt and pepper

Fish Patties
- 1 package (16 ounces, or 454 g) super-firm tofu
- Neutral oil for frying

Flour Dredge
- ¼ cup (32 g) all-purpose flour
- 1 teaspoon baking powder
- 2 teaspoons (5 g) Old Bay seasoning
- 2 tablespoons (24 g) kelp granules

Vegan Buttermilk
- ⅔ cup (160 ml) unsweetened plant milk
- 1 tablespoon (15 ml) apple cider vinegar
- 1 tablespoon (15 ml) lemon juice
- 1 teaspoon yellow miso

Bread Crumb Dredge
- 1½ cups (75 g) panko bread crumbs
- 2 teaspoons (5 g) Old Bay seasoning
- ½ teaspoon onion powder
- ½ teaspoon garlic powder
- ½ teaspoon salt

Assembly
- Burger buns
- 3 slices vegan cheese

SAUCE BOSS

Instead of a standard tartar sauce, spice it up and add a little Wasabi paste to it!

Or you can make one of my new favorite sauces which I call Old Bayo!
- 3/4 cup (170 g) Vegan Mayo
- 1/4 cup (60 ml) Frank's Hot Sauce
- 1 teaspoon Old Bay Seasoning
- 1 teaspoon lemon juice

Just whisk that together and slather on the sandwich to your heart's desire!

INSTRUCTIONS

Tartar Sauce

To make the tartar sauce, simply combine everything in a small bowl. Taste and adjust for seasoning. This stuff is so good, I could drink it!

Fish Patties

1. Cut the block of tofu into thirds, and if desired, cut them into perfect squares and make fish fingers with the excess tofu. Set aside.

2. Prepare the dredging stations: Add the flour dredge ingredients to a large bowl. To a separate bowl, add the vegan buttermilk ingredients and stir to combine. Add the panko bread crumbs to a large bowl; crush the panko in a blender or food processor for a finer breading, if desired. Stir in the bread crumb seasonings.

3. Heat a large pot of neutral oil (e.g., peanut, vegetable, or canola) to 375°F (190°C). While that heats up dredge the fish patties in the flour, then the vegan buttermilk, and in the panko bread crumbs. For a thicker breading, dredge again in the buttermilk and bread crumbs again.

4. Once the oil is up to temperature, carefully add the tofu fish patties. Fry for 3 to 5 minutes, or until they are beautifully golden brown. Let them rest on a wire rack.

Assembly

Toast the burger buns in a bit of oil in a medium skillet. To melt the cheese, flip the bottom bun, immediately add the cheese and cover. Once melted, assemble the sandwich by adding the tofu fish patty, a good slathering of the tartar sauce, and then the top bun!

PANDA EXPRESS
KUNG PAO CHICKEN

Ages ago, I used to work at a video game company, and we would often work late hours toward the end of a project. The company would often order us Panda Express for dinner, and while it was a nice gesture, it might have come from this restaurant a little too often. (Yes, I eventually burned out on it.) That being said, like just about everything in this book, the homemade rendition of this dish is better than I remember. (Then again, I might be biased as probably any food tastes better when it's not eaten at the end of a twelve-hour workday.)

YIELD: 3 TO 4 SERVINGS

INGREDIENTS

Chick'n
- 1 pound (454 g) vegan chick'n, chopped (see page 20)
- 3 tablespoons (45 ml) soy sauce
- 2 teaspoons (6 g) cornstarch
- 1 tablespoon (15 ml) Shaoxing cooking wine

Sauce
- ¼ cup (60 ml) vegan chicken stock
- 1 tablespoon (15 ml) rice vinegar
- 1 tablespoon (15 ml) Shaoxing cooking wine
- 2 tablespoons (28 ml) soy sauce
- 1 tablespoon (15 ml) vegan oyster sauce
- 1 tablespoon (15 ml) black vinegar
- 2 tablespoons (26 g) sugar
- 1–2 teaspoons (3–6 g) cornstarch

Stir-Fry
- Neutral oil for cooking
- 1 medium-size zucchini, cut into large dice
- 1 medium-size red bell pepper, cut into large dice
- 3 green onions, sliced (greens reserved)
- 6 dried chiles (Tien Tsin peppers or chile de arbol)
- 1 teaspoon minced fresh ginger
- 5 cloves garlic, minced
- ½ teaspoon ground sichuan pepper
- ⅓ cup (48 g) lightly salted roasted peanuts

Assembly
- Cooked rice or noodles
- Sesame seeds

INSTRUCTIONS

Chick'n

Marinate chick'n in the soy sauce, cornstarch, and Shaoxing wine for 20 to 30 minutes.

Sauce

Combine everything except the cornstarch in a small bowl. Set aside.

Stir-Fry

1. In a wok or wide skillet, heat up 2 to 3 tablespoons (28 to 45 ml) of a neutral oil over medium-high heat. Once the oil is hot, add the vegan chick'n, in batches if necessary, and stir-fry until lightly golden brown. Remove it from the pan and reserve for later.

2. Add the zucchini and bell pepper to the wok. Stir-fry for 1 to 2 minutes, or until they start to soften. Add the white part of the green onions and dried chiles. Stir-fry for 1 minute, then add the ginger, garlic, sichuan pepper, and peanuts. Stir-fry for 1 minute making sure not to burn the garlic. Add the vegan chick'n back in.

3. Quickly add 1 teaspoon of the cornstarch to the stir-fry sauce and whisk to combine. Add the sauce to the pan and stir-fry ensuring total sauce coverage on everything. Stir-fry for 1 minute, add 1 more teaspoon of cornstarch to thicken the sauce even more.

Assembly

Remove from the heat and serve immediately over rice or noodles. Garnish with green onions and sesame seeds. Enjoy!

CONTINUED

FINGER

FOODS

CHAPTER 4

WENDY'S CHICKEN NUGGETS

These are some of the best fast-food nuggets around, thanks to a combo wet-dry batter. Of course, what would these nuggets be without a vegan S'Awesome® sauce? It's a bit of a condiment party, and as I was putting it together for the first time, I was dubious. However, it's ridiculously good and once you dip a nugget. I think you'll agree it's out of this world!

YIELD: 24 NUGGETS AND ABOUT ¾ CUP (175 ML) SAUCE

INGREDIENTS

Sauce

- ¼ cup (60 ml) vegan ranch, store-bought or homemade (page 35)
- ¼ cup (60 ml) BBQ Sauce (page 35)
- 1 tablespoon (15 ml) hot sauce
- 2 teaspoons (10 g) Dijon mustard
- 2 teaspoons (8 g) yellow mustard
- 2 teaspoons (14 g) maple syrup
- ½ teaspoon vegan Worcestershire sauce
- ⅛ xanthan gum (optional)

Nuggets

- 1 pound (454 g) vegan chick'n (see page 20)
- Neutral oil for cooking

Wet Batter

- 1¼ cups (295 ml) water
- 1 cup (125 g) all-purpose flour
- 3 tablespoons (45 ml) unsweetened plant milk
- 1 tablespoon (15 ml) apple cider vinegar
- 2 tablespoons (28 ml) hot sauce
- 1 teaspoon salt

Dry Batter

- 1 cup (50 g) panko bread crumbs
- ½ cup (64 g) all-purpose flour
- ½ cup (64 g) cornstarch
- 1 tablespoon (14 g) baking powder
- 1 tablespoon (7 g) smoked paprika
- 2 tablespoons (14 g) garlic powder
- 2 tablespoons (14 g) onion powder
- 1 tablespoon (6 g) black pepper
- 1 tablespoon (17 g) salt
- 2 teaspoons (4 g) white pepper

INSTRUCTIONS

Sauce

Combine everything in a blender, adjust seasoning to taste. If desired, add ⅛ teaspoon xanthan gum while blending to thicken. Refrigerate at least 30 minutes.

Nuggets

1. Divide chick'n into ½-ounce (15-g) nuggets.

2. In a large bowl, combine all the ingredients for the wet batter. Whisk until it's a thick pancake batter consistency.

3. To make the dry batter, add the panko bread crumbs to a food processor. Pulse and blend until they are about half as big. Add the bread crumbs and remaining ingredients for the dry batter to another large bowl and whisk to incorporate.

4. Add enough neutral oil (e.g., peanut, vegetable, or canola) to cover the nuggets to a large Dutch oven or deep fryer. Heat the oil to 375°F (190°C).

5. Once the oil is up to temperature, dredge the nuggets in the wet batter, making sure to completely cover them (no dry spots). Shake off excess batter, then dredge them in the dry batter, ensuring total coverage. Shake off the excess dry batter, then carefully add the nuggets to the oil.

6. Fry them for 3 to 4 minutes, or until golden brown. Let rest for 2–3 minutes on a wire rack. Serve immediately with the sauce!

BUFFALO WILD WINGS BONELESS WINGS WITH MANGO HABANERO

Whenever I got these, I have to admit, I got the boneless wings. Even before going vegan, bones freaked me out! I would usually mix up my order, but I *always* got the mango habanero wings. Spicy and sweet is one of my favorite flavor combos, and this recipe has it in spades! Personally, I prefer dipping the wings in the sauce as opposed to saucing them for two reasons. One, the breading will retain its crispiness much better if you dip them. And two, you can have other dipping sauces to choose from! Dipping these in Vegan Ranch (page 35) or some BBQ Sauce (page 35) is also a totally good move!

YIELD: 15 TO 20 CHICK'N WINGS

INGREDIENTS

Sauce

- 1 mango or 12 ounces (340 g) frozen mango cubes, thawed
- 3–4 habanero peppers
- ½ onion (about 5 ounces, or 142 g)
- 2–3 cloves garlic, peeled
- 1 tablespoon (15 ml) lime juice
- ¼ cup (60 ml) Frank's RedHot® (original) sauce
- ¼ cup (60 ml) light corn syrup
- ¼ cup (85 g) maple syrup
- 2 teaspoons (12 g) salt
- ¼ cup (55 g) vegan butter

Wings

- 15–20 ounces (425–567 g) vegan chick'n (page 20)
- Neutral oil for cooking

Dry Batter

- ½ cup (64 g) all-purpose flour
- ½ cup (64 g) cornstarch
- 1 tablespoon (14 g) baking powder
- 1 tablespoon (7 g) smoked paprika
- 2 teaspoons (12 g) salt
- 1 teaspoon white pepper
- 1 tablespoon (7 g) garlic powder
- 1 tablespoon (7 g) onion powder
- Black pepper

Wet Batter

- 1 cup (235 ml) unsweetened plant milk
- 1 tablespoon (15 ml) apple cider vinegar
- 1 tablespoon (15 ml) hot sauce
- ⅓ cup (42 g) all-purpose flour

INSTRUCTIONS

Sauce

Blend all the ingredients except the vegan butter in a high-speed blender until smooth. Optionally, strain through a fine-mesh strainer to remove any fibrous bits. Add the sauce to a medium skillet over medium heat and bring to a boil. Reduce the heat and simmer for 20 minutes until it is reduced to half its volume (around 8 ounces, or 235 ml). Add the vegan butter and whisk until melted. Taste and adjust for seasoning, then set aside.

Wings

1. Form 15–20 (1 ounce, or 28 g) chick'n wings. Prepare the dredging stations by combining the ingredients for each batter in separate large bowls.

2. Heat a large pot of neutral oil (e.g., peanut, vegetable, or canola) to 375°F (190°C).

3. Once the oil is heated, dredge your wings in the dry batter, then the wet batter, and then back into the dry batter. Shake off any excess flour and batter and be sure to get total coverage on each phase.

4. You can fry these five or six at a time, just don't overcrowd them. Place the wings carefully in oil and fry for 4 to 5 minutes, until golden brown. Let them rest on a cooling rack.

5. If glazing the wings with the sauce, heat up the sauce and brush it on the wings while they are still hot. If using the sauce as a dipping sauce, serve immediately with the sauce. Enjoy!

JACK IN THE BOX STUFFED JALAPEÑOS

For non-vegans in the know, these jalapeños are a mandatory add-on to any order. There is nothing like the combo of spicy, cheesy, and crunchy. Now with this recipe, you get all the same components but totally vegan. The secret to success is that unlike a lot of jalapeño poppers, these aren't filled with a cream cheese–based mixture. Instead, they rely on a vegan cheese sauce that's liquid at room temp but firms up in the fridge—meaning it will fry up perfectly.

YIELD: 32 STUFFED JALAPEÑOS

INGREDIENTS

Cheese Filling
▶ 2 batches of Easy Cheese Sauce (page 33)

Jalapeños
▶ 16 medium jalapeño peppers
▶ Neutral oil for cooking

Wet Batter
▶ 1¼ cups (295 ml) water
▶ 1¼ cups (157 g) all-purpose flour
▶ 3 tablespoons (45 ml) unsweetened plant milk
▶ 3 tablespoons (45 ml) pickled jalapeño brine
▶ 1 teaspoon salt

Dry Batter
▶ 1 cup (50 g) panko bread crumbs
▶ ½ cup (64 g) all-purpose flour
▶ ½ cup (64 g) cornstarch
▶ 1 tablespoon (14 g) baking powder
▶ 1 tablespoon (7 g) smoked paprika
▶ 1 tablespoon (5 g) cayenne pepper
▶ 2 tablespoons (14 g) garlic powder
▶ 2 tablespoons (14 g) onion powder
▶ 1 tablespoon (17 g) salt

Serving
▶ Vegan ranch, store-bought or homemade (page 35)

INSTRUCTIONS

Cheese Filling

Prepare two batches of Easy Cheese Sauce (page 33). Once the cheese sauce is well melted and combined, transfer it to a reusable container, seal it, and refrigerate it for at least 2 hours, or preferably overnight.

Jalapeños

1. Once the cheese sauce has cooled, slice the jalapeños in half lengthwise and take out the seeds and ribs. Fill each jalapeño with a heaping tablespoon (20 ml) of the cheese mixture. Set aside.

2. In a large bowl, combine all the ingredients for the wet batter. Whisk until it's a thick pancake batter consistency. To make the dry batter, add the panko bread crumbs to a food processor, and pulse and blend until they are about half as big. Add the bread crumbs and remaining ingredients for the dry batter to another large bowl and whisk to incorporate.

3. Add neutral oil (e.g., peanut, vegetable, or canola) to a large Dutch oven or deep fryer. Do not fill it up past the halfway point. Heat the oil to 375°F (190°C).

4. Once the oil is up to temperature, dredge the peppers in the wet batter, ensuring no dry spots. Shake off the excess batter, then dredge them in the dry batter. Again, with total coverage, shake off the excess dry batter, then carefully add them to the oil.

5. Fry them for 3 to 4 minutes, or until golden brown and crispy. Add them to a wire rack lined baking sheet to cool down.

Serving

Once the peppers have been fried, dip them in some vegan ranch and enjoy!

SONIC
CHILI CHEESE
TOTS

My wife is from Texas, so I had her taste test these against her fast-food memories from the place with skating servers. Her verdict: would order again and again. These tots pack a ton of flavor (which is great because that's kind of the point of this whole book). Have extra chili? I've found this recipe works well on just about anything: fries, hot dogs, burgers, you name it.

YIELD: 4 TO 6 SERVINGS

INGREDIENTS

Tater Tots
▶ 1 bag (32 ounces, or 907 g) frozen tater tots

Chili
▶ 1 tablespoon (16 g) chipotles in adobo
▶ 3 tablespoons (23 g) chili seasoning
▶ 1 tablespoon (7 g) ground cumin
▶ 1 tablespoon (7 g) smoked paprika
▶ 1 tablespoon (7 g) masa harina
▶ 1 medium onion
▶ Neutral oil for cooking
▶ 1 pound (454 g) plant-based meat

▶ 3 cloves garlic, minced
▶ 1 tablespoon (15 ml) pickled jalapeño brine
▶ 1 cup (235 ml) beefless broth
▶ 1 can (8 ounces, or 226 g) tomato sauce
▶ Salt and pepper

Assembly
▶ 1 batch of Easy Cheese Sauce (page 33)
▶ Chopped onions
▶ Pickled jalapeños

INSTRUCTIONS

Tater Tots

Preheat the oven and cook the tater tots according to the package instructions. An entire bag should take about 30 minutes—which is around the same time it takes to throw the chili and cheese sauce together, so everything should time out perfectly.

Chili

1. Mix all the dry seasonings together first. Quarter the onion and add it to a food processor. Blitz it until it's pureed.

2. Heat up a large saucepan over medium heat and add 1 tablespoon (15 ml) of neutral oil. Once the oil is heated, add the plant-based meat and crumble. Cook for 4 to 5 minutes until all the pink is gone and it's browned a bit. Add the onion puree and stir to combine. Cook for 3 to 4 minutes.

3. Add the garlic and stir to combine, cooking for only 1 minute or so. Add the rest of the ingredients, including the seasonings, and stir to combine. Taste and adjust for seasoning, then reduce until the chili is thick enough that a wooden spoon can run along the bottom of the pan and create a clear path for a couple seconds. For a thinner chili, reduce for less time and add more water if necessary.

Assembly

Once the tots are done, add them to a plate and cover them with plenty of the chili and cheese sauce. Top it with chopped onions, pickled jalapeños, or any other toppings and dig in!

FIVE GUYS
CAJUN STYLE
FRIES

What would a fast-food book be without a delicious recipe for fries! Five Guys fries are one of the more popular fast-food items of recent memory. And that's because their fries are made fresh and seasoned to perfection with Cajun spices. They are also vegan so this was a rare opportunity for me to actually contrast and compare with the real thing. I can confidently say that this homemade version is just as good, if not better!

YIELD: 3 TO 4 SERVINGS

INGREDIENTS

Cajun Seasoning
- 2 teaspoons (12 g) salt
- 2 teaspoons (4 g) garlic powder
- 2 teaspoons (5 g) smoked paprika

- ½ teaspoon black pepper
- ½ teaspoon onion powder
- 1 teaspoon cayenne pepper
- ½ teaspoon white pepper

Fries
- 3 pounds (1.4 kg) russet potatoes
- 4–5 cups (1–1.2 L) peanut oil for frying

INSTRUCTIONS

Cajun Seasoning

Combine all the ingredients in a small bowl and set it aside.

Fries

1. To ensure uniform fries, choose potatoes that are the same size; 5 inches (13 cm) long is ideal. Wash them well, but don't peel them!

2. A French fry press is ideal for cutting fries, but cutting them by hand can be done in a jiffy as well. Cut the potatoes into planks about ½ inch (1 cm) thick. Cut each plank into sticks (or fries) about ½ inch (1 cm) thick. There you go, fresh-cut fries! Let them soak in cold water for 30 minutes. Then, drain and dry them.

3. Frying these up will take place in two stages. First, they'll be fried for about 3 minutes at 300° to 325°F (150° to 165°C). Next, they'll rest on a wire rack until all the other fries have been fried. The second phase will entail raising the heat to 350° to 375°F (175° to 190°C) and frying again, this time until golden brown.

4. The oil needs to be in that range for both those phases. If it dips below (300°F [150°C]) on the first fry, there's a risk of getting soggy fries. And if it goes too high, there's risk of overcooking the outside and undercooking the inside. It's imperative that the temperature is in that range.

5. Overcrowding the pan will cause the oil to drop too much. Do this in batches. Even when adding a proper number of fries, the oil temperature will drop. Heat the oil up to 340° to 350°F (171° to 175°C) before adding fries for the first batch, and around 390°F (199°C) for the second. That way the oil will drop, but still be in the range that's optimum.

CONTINUED

INSTRUCTIONS

6. Frying a few test fries by themselves to figure out the desired doneness is recommended. The second phase of frying should only take about 5 minutes per batch, at which point the fries will start to get golden brown toward the ends, but the middle will still be a bit pale. Frying until the fries are completely golden brown results in an overdone French fry.

7. Once fried, add them to a wire rack to drain for 30 seconds or so. Then toss them in a large bowl with the Cajun seasoning, shaking the bowl and tossing the fries around. This will help ensure an even distribution of seasoning!

NOTE: Skip the Cajun seasoning and simply salt the fries after the second fry for regular fries!

THE BURGERS

Five Guys burgers are fairly simple and that's the beauty of 'em! The thing that makes their burgers special is the number of toppings available, which you can customize to your heart's content!

Here's the list of toppings. Go ahead and create your own masterpiece! I used to get bacon, jalapeños, grilled onions, lettuce, tomato, mayo, mustard, and ketchup.

Five Guys Toppings: Mayo, lettuce, pickles, tomatoes, grilled onions, grilled mushrooms, ketchup, mustard, relish, onions, jalapeños, green peppers, Bar-B-Que sauce, hot sauce, and A.1.™ steak sauce.

THE CHEESECAKE FACTORY FRIED MAC 'N' CHEESE

This is one of those places that I used to go on my lunch break when I worked in an office, especially on a Friday when a few friends and I wanted to take a longer lunch. We always ordered these and honestly, I wished I would've just ordered a whole plate for myself. Whenever we were eating, it was always me who would hurry up and then eat an extra one while the other folks were still finishing up their first piece. Yeah, maybe it was rude, but it was delicious! This recipe makes a lot, so feel free to cut the recipe in half—unless you're like me and want to eat an entire plate yourself!

YIELD: 10 MAC 'N' CHEESE BALLS

CONTINUED

INGREDIENTS

Mac 'n' Cheese

- 8 ounces (226 g) macaroni
- 5 tablespoons (70 g) vegan butter
- 6 tablespoons (48 g) all-purpose flour
- 2½ cups (570 ml) unsweetened plant milk
- 10 ounces (283 g) shredded vegan cheese
- ½ teaspoon onion powder
- ½ teaspoon garlic powder
- ½ teaspoon salt
- 1 teaspoon mushroom seasoning
- Neutral oil for cooking

Frying

Dry Dredge

- 1 cup (120 g) flour
- 1 teaspoon onion powder
- 1 teaspoon garlic powder
- 1 teaspoon salt
- 2 teaspoons (5 g) Italian seasoning

Wet Dredge

- 2 cups (475 ml) unsweetened plant milk
- 2 tablespoons (28 ml) apple cider vinegar

Bread Crumbs

- 2½ cups (290 g) bread crumbs
- ¼ cup (20 g) vegan parmesan
- 1 teaspoon garlic powder
- 1 teaspoon onion powder
- Salt

Plating

- Marinara sauce
- Vegan parmesan
- Chopped fresh Italian parsley

NOTE: For the mac 'n' cheese, I don't recommend using the Easy Cheese Sauce (page 33). I found it didn't have enough of a binding effect, and I couldn't get these to hold their shape. The recipe here, a more traditional cheese sauce, will do the trick!

INSTRUCTIONS

Mac 'n' Cheese

1. Cook the macaroni according to the package instructions. To make the cheese sauce, melt the vegan butter in a large saucepan over medium heat. Once melted, add the flour 1 tablespoon (8 g) at a time and whisk to combine between each tablespoon. When all flour has been incorporated cook down for 1 minute to get rid of the raw flour.

2. Whisk in the plant milk, ½ cup (120 ml) at a time. Then, add the cheese and seasonings, and whisk until the cheese fully melts. Taste and adjust for seasoning. Fold the sauce into the cooked macaroni.

3. Add the mac 'n' cheese to a casserole dish and refrigerate for 2 hours or overnight. Then, scoop ¼ cup (about 50 g) of the mac 'n' cheese and form it into a ball. Place it on a wax paper–lined baking sheet or a lightly greased muffin pan. Repeat until all of the mac 'n' cheese has been formed into balls. Place the baking sheet or muffin pan in the freezer for 20 minutes. Be careful not to freeze them too long or they'll still be cold after frying.

Frying

1. Prepare the dredging station by adding and combine the ingredients in separate bowls for the dry dredge, the wet dredge, and the bread crumbs. Bring a large pot of neutral oil (such as vegetable, canola, or peanut) up to 350°F (175°C or gas mark 4).

2. Dredge the mac 'n' cheese balls in the dry dredge, the wet dredge, and then into the bread crumbs. Repeat a dredge into the wet dredge and bread crumbs and then carefully add to the pot of oil.

3. Fry for 3 minutes, or until the entire ball is golden brown and crispy. Move the ball around and ensure it gets evenly fried, especially if the oil doesn't full cover it. Once fried to perfection, add to a wire rack–lined baking sheet to cool.

Plating

Once all the balls have been fried, add a nice layer of marinara sauce to a plate. Add four of the balls, then grate over some vegan parmesan and add some parsley on top. Eat them with a knife and fork, or go ahead and grab 'em and eat them like an apple! Either way, enjoy!

RED LOBSTER CHEDDAR BAY BISCUITS®

I remember the first time I went to this seafood-heavy chain. All I'd ever heard was people raving about these biscuits. So naturally, I ordered them . . . and ate about ten of them, which meant I had absolutely no room for whatever main dish I ordered. I have no regrets about it! Well, except for the fact that they weren't vegan. However, the biscuits you see here are, and from my memory these are just as good. And with this recipe size, you can eat about ten, just like I did!

YIELD: 10 BISCUITS

INGREDIENTS

Biscuits (Dry)

▶ 2 cups (240 g) all-purpose flour
▶ 1 tablespoon (14 g) baking powder
▶ 1 tablespoon (13 g) sugar
▶ 1 tablespoon (5 g) nutritional yeast
▶ 1 teaspoon garlic powder
▶ ½ teaspoon onion powder
▶ ¼ teaspoon Old Bay seasoning
▶ ¼ teaspoon cayenne pepper
▶ 1 teaspoon dried parsley
▶ ½ teaspoon salt
▶ 4 ounces (113 g) shredded vegan cheddar cheese

Biscuits (Wet)

▶ 1 cup (235 ml) unsweetened plant milk
▶ 1 tablespoon (15 ml) apple cider vinegar
▶ ½ cup (112 g) vegan butter, melted

Topping

▶ ¼ cup (55 g) vegan butter, melted
▶ ½ teaspoon garlic powder
▶ 1 tablespoon (4 g) chopped fresh Italian parsley
▶ Pinch of salt

INSTRUCTIONS

Biscuits

1. Preheat the oven to 425°F (220°C or gas mark 7). Combine all the dry ingredients in one large bowl, and the wet ingredients in another large bowl. Then, dump the wet ingredients into the bowl of dry ingredients. Gently fold them together until just mixed. Careful not to overmix!

2. Line a baking sheet with parchment paper, then scoop out ¼ cup (60 ml) of the biscuit batter and drop it onto the baking sheet. Repeat with the rest of the batter, leaving 2 inches (5 cm) between each biscuit as they will expand when cooking.

3. Once all biscuits have been dropped, bake them for 12 to 14 minutes, or until golden brown.

Topping

Whisk together the butter, garlic powder, parsley, and salt. Brush it liberally on each biscuit while it's still hot. Serve immediately and enjoy!

SONIC ONION RINGS

I wanted to include onion rings in this book, and when researching I found out these are some of the most popular ones out there. While you'd think onion rings would be easy to make vegan, not so with these. Are they fried with meat or flavored with meat? Nope! But they are apparently dredged in melted vanilla ice cream! I tested this with vegan equivalents and wasn't super stoked about the results. They were too sweet for me, and this was a common complaint among those I shared them with. So, to get more control over the sweetness I experimented with various ratios of plant milk and maple syrup instead. I gotta' say these really hit the spot, and they aren't too sweet even if you dip 'em in some BBQ sauce! Enjoy these with a Cherry Limeade (page 158) for the full experience!

YIELD: 4 TO 6 SERVINGS

INGREDIENTS

Onion Rings
- 2 large, sweet onions (about 2 pounds [907 g])
- Neutral oil for cooking

Dry Batter
- 1 cup (120 g) all-purpose flour
- ½ cup (60 g) cornstarch
- 1–2 teaspoons (6–12 g) salt
- ½–1 teaspoon cayenne pepper

Wet Batter
- 1 cup (235 ml) unsweetened plant milk
- 2 teaspoons (10 ml) vanilla extract
- ¼ cup (85 g) maple syrup

Bread Crumbs
- 1½–2 cups (170–230 g) bread crumbs

Serving
- BBQ sauce or vegan ranch, store-bought or homemade (page 35)

INSTRUCTIONS

Onion Rings

1. Slice the onions into ½-inch (1-cm)-thick slices and let them rest in a large bowl of ice water. Prepare the dredging stations: Combine the ingredients for the dry batter in one large bowl, and the ingredients for the wet batter in a second large bowl. Add the bread crumbs to a third large bowl.

2. Add some neutral oil to a large pot or Dutch oven and heat the oil to 350° to 360°F (175° to 182°C). Dry off the onions, and then dredge them in the wet batter, then the dry, shaking off the excess each time. Dredge again in the wet batter, and then dredge them in the bread crumbs. Thoroughly coat them and shake off any excess.

3. Carefully add the onions to the oil and fry in small batches, making sure to not overcrowd the pot. Fry for 2 to 3 minutes, or until beautifully golden browned. Let them rest on a wire rack and season with salt immediately while still hot

Serving

Once they are done, serve them with some BBQ sauce or vegan ranch!

TGI FRIDAYS MOZZARELLA STICKS

Whenever dining in at this place, I always got the appetizer sampler, and these cheese sticks were a big reason for sure! Thanks to new cheese options, vegan mozzarella sticks have come a long way since I've been vegan. Even store-bought ones can be good these days. However, this recipe is for the best mozzarella sticks I've ever had! I will admit that there are a few uncommon ingredients (for more info check out page 27), but they all do their part to make this cheese super stretchy and gooey. These are fantastic on their own but dipping them in some marinara or vegan ranch takes them to another level. Don't skip the dip!

YIELD: 12 TO 16 STICKS

INGREDIENTS

Mozzarella Cheese

- ▶ ¼ cup (34 g) raw cashews
- ▶ Boiling water for soaking
- ▶ 2 teaspoons (5 g) psyllium husk powder plus ¼ cup (60 ml) cool water
- ▶ 1½ cups (355 ml) unsweetened plant milk
- ▶ ¼ cup (54 g) refined coconut oil, melted
- ▶ 1½ teaspoons lactic acid
- ▶ 1 teaspoon salt
- ▶ 2 tablespoons (15 g) tapioca starch
- ▶ 1½ tablespoons (15 g) kappa carrageenan
- ▶ Neutral oil for cooking

Frying
Dry Dredge

- ▶ ⅓ cup (42 g) all-purpose flour
- ▶ ½ teaspoon onion powder
- ▶ ½ teaspoon garlic powder
- ▶ ½ teaspoon salt
- ▶ 1 teaspoon Italian seasoning

Wet Dredge

- ▶ 1¼ cups (295 ml) unsweetened plant milk
- ▶ 1 tablespoon (15 ml) apple cider vinegar

Bread Crumbs

- ▶ 2 cups (230 g) bread crumbs
- ▶ 3 tablespoons (15 g) vegan parmesan crumbles
- ▶ ½ teaspoon garlic powder
- ▶ ½ teaspoon onion powder
- ▶ ½ teaspoon salt

Serving

- ▶ Marinara
- ▶ Vegan ranch, store-bought or homemade (page 35)

FROM APPETIZER TO MAIN COURSE

Feel free to add these on top of a burger, or you can even make a monster grilled cheese with them!

CONTINUED

INSTRUCTIONS

Mozzarella Cheese

1. Cover the cashews in boiling water for 10 minutes. Combine the psyllium husk powder and cool water for 5 minutes, until thickened.

2. Now, this part is important: Once this process starts, it cannot stop. Make sure to have everything set up for speed and efficiency.

3. Have a silicone or glass container ready next to the blender. Heat the plant milk until just boiling. Quickly but carefully add the hot plant milk to the blender, and then add everything EXCEPT the tapioca starch and kappa carrageenan and oil. Blend on high speed until smooth, quickly taste and adjust for seasoning. While the blender is still going, add the tapioca starch followed by the kappa carrageenan. This is where SCIENCE happens. Once the kappa reacts to the heat in the plant milk it will begin to solidify. If the blender starts to sound like it's having a hard time, that's a good sign that it's setting, and it's time to quickly transfer to a silicone mold or glass container. Refrigerate for at least 4 hours. After that, it should be firm enough to grate. If not, pop it in the freezer for 15 to 20 minutes.

4. Slice the mozzarella into sticks and set them aside in the fridge.

Frying

1. Prepare the dredging station: Combine the dry ingredients in a large bowl, and the wet and bread crumb ingredients in two large bowls. Fill a large pot or Dutch oven with about 2 to 3 inches (5 to 7.5 cm) of a neutral oil (e.g., peanut, vegetable, or canola). Heat the oil to 360° to 375°F (182° to 190°C).

2. Dredge each mozzarella stick in the wet, then the dry, then back into the wet, and then lastly into the bread crumbs. Make sure to coat thoroughly and shake off the excess each time. Gently and carefully add three to four mozzarella sticks to the pot of oil. Make sure not to crowd it. After 2 to 3 minutes, or when the sticks are beautifully golden brown, remove them from the oil. Let them rest on a wire rack.

Serving

Let the mozzarella sticks cool for 5 to 10 minutes, then serve with some marinara or vegan ranch for dipping!

LITTLE CAESARS CRAZY BREAD®

Chances are you knew someone at some point who was hooked on the inexpensive pizza from this place . . . and, if so, you probably either tried it or snagged one of these signature breadsticks. While the flavor of these may take you back, I admit I did dial in this recipe to be a little less greasy. Even so, I honestly had to restrain myself from eating all of these once I made them so I could actually take a photo for the book. They were super good on their own, but once I dipped them in some marinara it was ridiculously tasty. Who needs the pizza?

YIELD: 16 PIECES

CONTINUED

INGREDIENTS

Bread

▶ 4 cups (480 g) bread flour, plus more as needed

▶ 2¼ teaspoons (7 g) instant yeast

▶ 2 tablespoons (26 g) sugar

▶ 2 teaspoons (12 g) salt

▶ 1 teaspoon garlic powder

▶ 1½ cups (355 ml) water, heated to 110°F (43°C)

▶ 2 tablespoons (28 ml) olive oil, plus more for preparing the bowl

Garlic Butter

▶ ¼ cup (55 g) vegan butter, melted

▶ 1 teaspoon garlic powder

▶ ½ teaspoon salt

▶ ¼ cup (20 g) vegan parmesan, finely grated

Serving

▶ Vegan parmesan

▶ Marinara or vegan ranch, store-bought or homemade (page 35)

INSTRUCTIONS

Bread

1. In the bowl of a stand mixer, combine the bread flour, instant yeast, sugar, salt, and garlic powder. Using the dough hook, turn the stand mixer on low speed and add the water and oil. Once the wet and dry have combined turn the speed up to medium and let it mix for 7 to 8 minutes. The dough should be tacky but not too sticky, so if it's sticking to the side of the bowl, add 1 tablespoon (8 g) of flour at a time until it pulls away and forms a dough ball.

2. Lightly grease a large bowl. Add the dough ball, and cover with a kitchen towel or plastic wrap. Let the dough rise for 1½ hours, or until doubled in size.

Baking the Bread

Preheat the oven to 425°F (220°C). Remove the towel or plastic wrap from the bowl, and gently deflate the dough ball by hand. On a well-floured surface, dump the ball out of the bowl. Cut it in half, and then cut each half into eight equal-size pieces. Using floured hands, roll each piece into a long, thin loaf of bread, like a mini-baguette. Add them to a parchment-lined baking sheet, keeping them 2 inches (5 cm) apart. Bake the rolls for 6 to 7 minutes.

Garlic Butter

In the meantime, make the garlic butter by combining all the ingredients in a small bowl. Once the rolls have baked for 6 to 7 minutes, remove them from the oven, and brush on about half of the garlic butter mixture. Return them to the oven for 5 to 6 minutes, or until slightly golden brown.

Serving

Remove the rolls from the oven, brush them with the rest of the garlic butter, and sprinkle on more vegan parmesan. Dip in some marinara or vegan ranch and enjoy!

BREAKFASTS

CHAPTER 5

**MCDONALD'S
MCMUFFIN**®

**TACO BELL
GRANDE SCRAMBLER
BURRITO**

**WHATABURGER
HONEY BUTTER
CHICKEN BISCUIT**

**BOJANGLES
SOUTHERN GRAVY
BISCUIT**

**CRACKER BARREL
HASH BROWN
CASSEROLE**

**MCDONALD'S
HASH BROWNS**

**IHOP
NEW YORK
CHEESECAKE
PANCAKES**

**BURGER KING
FRENCH TOAST
STICKS**

**WAFFLE HOUSE
APPLE CINNAMON
WAFFLE**

**STARBUCKS
PUMPKIN CREAM
CHEESE MUFFIN**

MCDONALD'S MCMUFFIN®

Before going vegan, this might have been my most-ordered item from the drive-thru. While not quite as easy as grabbing one from the window of your car, these are relatively convenient and make for a fun weekend treat. The savory seasoned sausage patties contrast perfectly with the umami-packed tofu egg.

YIELD: 3 SANDWICHES

INGREDIENTS

Tofu Egg

- 1 block (14 ounces, or 397 g) extra-firm tofu
- 1 tablespoon (5 g) nutritional yeast
- 1 teaspoon garlic powder
- 1 teaspoon onion powder
- ½ teaspoon mustard powder
- 1 teaspoon salt
- ¼ teaspoon black salt (kala namak)

Sausage Patties

- 12 ounces (340 g) plant-based meat
- 1 teaspoon garlic powder
- 1 teaspoon onion powder
- 1 teaspoon ground sage
- 1 teaspoon smoked paprika
- 2 teaspoons (10 g) packed brown sugar
- Pinch of ground cloves
- ½ teaspoon cayenne pepper
- ¼ teaspoon ground fennel (optional)
- Salt and pepper

Sandwiches

- Hash brown patty, store-bought or homemade (optional; page 134)
- Vegan butter
- 3 English muffins
- Nonstick cooking spray
- 3 slices vegan cheese

INSTRUCTIONS

Tofu Egg

Press the block of tofu for 20 minutes. Once pressed, slice the block into thirds. Then, use a cookie cutter the same radius as the English muffin to cut out an "egg" patty. In a rimmed dish, combine the seasonings for the tofu egg. Dip each tofu egg into the mixture and coat the bottom and top of each tofu egg patty. Set aside.

Sausage Patties

Combine all ingredients for the sausage patties in a large bowl and mix thoroughly until the seasoning is evenly distributed. Divide into three (4-oz, or 113-g) balls, and form into patties with a cookie cutter or burger press.

NOTE: If making a frozen hash brown, now would be a good time to cook it according to package instructions, so it'll be ready when everything else is done cooking.

CONTINUED

Sandwiches

1. Heat up a large skillet over medium heat. Spread some vegan butter on each of the English muffins and add them to the pan. Cook for 5 minutes, or until the butter has melted and the muffins become beautifully browned. Remove the muffins and set aside.

2. Keeping the pan over medium heat, spray it with some cooking spray and add the sausage patties. Cook on each side for 3 to 4 minutes, or until they develop a wonderful, caramelized crust. Set aside.

3. Immediately add the tofu egg patties to the pan. Cook for 2 to 3 minutes, or until the seasonings have browned and become aromatic. Flip and then quickly add a slice of vegan cheese to each one. Add 1 tablespoon (15 ml) of water to the pan and cover immediately to steam and melt the cheese.

4. After 3 minutes, the cheese should be melted to perfection. Assemble each sandwich as follows from bottom to top: bottom English muffin, condiment of choice (optional), frozen hash brown patty (optional), sausage patty, tofu egg, more condiment (optional), top English muffin.

NOTES AND SHORTCUTS:

▶ Use the leftover tofu scraps for a scramble or stir-fry.

▶ For an even easier vegan egg, use a store-bought pourable vegan egg product if you wish.

▶ The sausage patties can be made by seasoning my TVP Burger Patty recipe (page 14) with the sausage seasonings, or even use your favorite store-bought plant-based meat. You can also skip the sausage and make these with some Rice Paper Bacon (page 28)!

▶ I highly recommend upgrading by adding a Hash Brown (page 134)!

▶ For an upgrade, add any sauces or condiments of your choice, such as vegan mayo, aioli, or sriracha.

TACO BELL
GRANDE
SCRAMBLER
BURRITO

How much do I love breakfast burritos? Well, I'll have a breakfast burrito for dinner, that's how much I enjoy 'em! For this one, the tofu scramble is important but don't overlook the recipe for the amazing potatoes! I've made them several times and they go great with so many things! Add them to a Crunchwrap Supreme (page 66) or a Cheesy Gordita Crunch (page 68), too. Or just whip them up as part of a more traditional breakfast plate.

YIELD: 2 BURRITOS
(PLUS EXTRA TOFU SCRAMBLE)

CONTINUED

INGREDIENTS

Potatoes

- 1 pound (454 g) russet potatoes
- ¼ cup (32 g) all-purpose flour
- 1 tablespoon (7 g) Taco Seasoning (page 37)
- Neutral oil for cooking
- Salt

Tofu Scramble

- 1 block (14 ounces, or 397 g) medium-firm tofu
- ½ cup (58 g) shredded vegan cheese (optional)
- ¼–½ cup (60–120 ml) unsweetened plant milk, plus more as needed
- 2 tablespoons (10 g) nutritional yeast
- 1 teaspoon garlic salt
- ½ teaspoon onion powder
- ¼ teaspoon ground turmeric
- ¼ teaspoon smoked paprika
- ¼ teaspoon pepper
- Black salt (kala namak; optional)
- Neutral oil for cooking

Assembly

- 2 large flour tortillas
- 4–6 slices Rice Paper Bacon (page 38)
- ½ cup (120 ml) Easy Cheese Sauce (page 33)
- ⅓ cup (80 g) vegan sour cream, store-bought or homemade (page 86)

LEFTOVERS FOR LUNCH!

Like with the other Taco Bell recipes in this book, the leftovers are a winner, too! Why not use extra potatoes and cheese sauce to make some Cheesy Fiesta Potatoes? Or a spicy potato taco? You can even take the components of the this Burrito and the Hash Brown on page 134 to make a Breakfast Crunchwrap (why it's not called the Brunchwrap is beyond me).

INSTRUCTIONS

Potatoes

1. Wash and peel the potatoes, then wash them again. Dice the potatoes by slicing them into ½-inch (1-cm) French fry–shaped sticks, and then cubing each stick into ½-inch (1-cm) cubes.

2. Once the potatoes are diced, add them to a large bowl and cover with some water for 10 minutes. Drain and pat them dry. In a large bowl, combine the flour and taco seasoning. Toss the cubed potatoes in the seasoned flour until they are all thoroughly coated.

3. Add neutral oil (e.g., peanut, vegetable, or canola) to a large, deep rimmed skillet or Dutch oven. Bring it up to between 350° and 375°F (175° and 190°C).

4. Fry the potatoes in batches, careful not to overcrowd the pan. Fry for 8 to 10 minutes, until golden brown. Let them rest on a wire rack, and sprinkle with salt immediately.

NOTE: Feel free to double the potatoes for leftovers! They reheat well, just panfry or air-fry them until heated through.

Tofu Scramble

1. Pat the tofu dry with paper or tea towels. Gently squeeze out any excess liquid. Press the tofu for at least 20 minutes in a tofu press or using something heavy such as a cast-iron skillet. Crumble the tofu into a large mixing bowl. For a finer texture, crumble with the back of a fork. Add all the seasoning (except the black salt) and mix until combined.

2. In a small skillet, heat up a little oil over medium heat. Add the tofu and cook for 2 minutes, stirring occasionally. Add the plant milk and mix. If a softer consistency is desired, add more milk. Cook until heated through, and always season to taste! Remove from the heat, and sprinkle with desired amount of black salt (if using).

NOTE: This makes a lot of leftover tofu scramble. Use it as a convenient breakfast or combine it with some of the other breakfast recipes in this book!

Assembly

1. Warm up the tortilla in the microwave for 30 seconds or on the stovetop in a dry skillet until warmed through. Place the tortilla on a flat work surface, add a generous amount of the tofu scramble, followed by a nice heaping helping of potatoes. Chop up the vegan bacon and sprinkle that over, followed by a good old drizzling of the vegan cheese sauce and the vegan sour cream.

2. Fold the ends of the tortilla over the filling, then carefully roll the tortilla up, like a burrito. Tuck in the ends. This isn't necessary, but it's totally recommended! Heat up a little oil in a skillet, then add the burrito seam-side down. Cook it for 3 minutes, or until golden brown, then flip on to the other side and cook for 3 minutes, or until golden brown. Enjoy!

WHATABURGER HONEY BUTTER CHICKEN BISCUIT

When I started veganizing my favorite fast-food meals, my wife (who's from Texas) requested I do one of her favorites from this Texas institution. And who am I to deny her that? I mean, it's not like she had to twist my arm: Who doesn't like fried chick'n on a biscuit with honey butter? This is by far one of the best things to come out of Texas, and it's truly an iconic sandwich that I'm happy to report is ridiculously delicious (even when it's vegan and made in California!).

**YIELD: 3 SANDWICHES
(PLUS EXTRA BISCUITS)**

INGREDIENTS

Biscuits

- 1 cup (235 ml) unsweetened plant milk
- 1 tablespoon (15 ml) apple cider vinegar
- 2½ cups (300 g) self-rising flour, plus more for dusting
- 1 teaspoon sugar
- ½ teaspoon salt
- 1 teaspoon nutritional yeast
- ½ cup (112 g) vegan butter, frozen
- 2 tablespoons (28 ml) melted vegan butter

Chick'n

- 9 ounces (255 g) vegan chick'n (page 20)
- Neutral oil for cooking

Dry Dredge

- ¼ cup (32 g) all-purpose flour
- ¼ cup (32 g) cornstarch
- ½ tablespoon (7 g) baking powder
- ½ teaspoon salt
- 1 teaspoon smoked paprika
- ½ teaspoon white pepper
- ½ teaspoon garlic powder
- ½ teaspoon onion powder
- ½ teaspoon black pepper

Wet Dredge

- ½ cup (120 ml) unsweetened plant milk
- ½ tablespoon (8 ml) apple cider vinegar
- ½ tablespoon (8 ml) hot sauce
- ½ teaspoon garlic powder
- ½ teaspoon onion powder
- ½ teaspoon salt

Honey Butter

- ½ cup (170 g) vegan honey (maple syrup, agave, etc.)
- ¼ cup (55 g) vegan butter, softened

INSTRUCTIONS

Biscuits

1. Preheat the oven to 450°F (230°C or gas mark 8).

2. Combine the plant milk and apple cider vinegar in a small bowl, let it sit for 5 minutes to thicken for a vegan buttermilk. Meanwhile, add the flour, sugar, salt, and nutritional yeast to a large bowl and stir to combine. Grate the frozen vegan butter into the dry ingredients, or use a pastry cutter or fork and break up the butter into pea-size pieces.

3. Make a well in the flour-butter mixture, then pour in the vegan buttermilk. Fold together with a wooden spoon until just mixed, being careful not to over work the dough. It will be quite shaggy. That's okay, it will come together with the next step!

4. Lay out the dough on a floured work surface and sprinkle a bit more flour onto the dough. With floured hands flatten it out, or rub some flour on a rolling pin and roll out the dough into a rectangle about ¾ to 1 inch (2 to 2.5 cm) thick. Fold the dough over itself like a letter for an envelope, so fold one-third over toward the center, then the other side over the

CONTINUED

rest of the dough. Gently flatten it by hand or rolling pin, turn it 90 degrees, and repeat that process four more times. Keep the flour handy in case the dough is still sticky.

5. Once the dough has been folded and flattened or rolled to ¾ inch (2 cm) thick, get a 3- or 3½-inch (7.5- or 9-cm) cookie cutter, lightly flour it, and cut out some biscuits. Don't twist the cookie cutter as this can prevent the biscuits from rising. Once all the available area has been cut out, take the scraps, reroll them, and cut out more biscuits. There should be six to eight depending on the size.

6. Add the biscuits to a parchment-lined baking sheet and make sure they are touching each other ever so slightly. This will help them rise as well! Throw them in the oven for 7 to 8 minutes, or until the tops start to brown. Pull them out and brush the tops with half of the melted vegan butter. Add them back into the oven for 5 minutes, or until the tops are golden brown. Remove from the oven and brush with the rest of the melted vegan butter.

Chick'n

1. Form three (3-oz, or 85-g) chick'n patties from the vegan chick'n the same size as the biscuits. If using thawed store-bought vegan chick'n, add the patties to a parchment-lined baking sheet and throw in the freezer for 1 hour to firm up.

2. Prepare the dredging stations by simply combining the ingredients for each batter in separate bowls.

3. Heat a large pot of neutral oil (e.g., peanut, vegetable, or canola) to 375°F (190°C).

4. Once the oil is up to 375°F (190°C), dredge your patties in the wet batter, then the dry batter, and then repeat for a double dredge. Shake off any excess flour and batter and be sure to get total coverage on each phase. Place carefully in the hot oil and fry for 4 to 5 minutes, until golden brown. Let them rest on a cooling rack.

Honey Butter

There are lots of options for the honey butter! Maple syrup, date syrup, and agave can all be used instead of bee honey. Heating the maple syrup or agave and reducing for a more honey-like texture is a good move, but it will still be super good without that step. For the honey butter, simply combine whatever vegan honey is desired with the butter—that's it!

Assembly

Add a fried chick'n patty to a biscuit, and drizzle generously with the honey butter. Add the top biscuit and ENJOY!

BOJANGLES SOUTHERN GRAVY BISCUIT

I couldn't do a breakfast chapter without biscuits and gravy, a recipe that is in my top five breakfasts of all time! The combination of buttery biscuits topped with savory gravy is unrivaled! These days vegan butter and vegan breakfast sausage have made so many advances that you won't be able to distinguish this from its non-vegan counterpart! That being said, feel free to leave out the sausage all together as this gravy is still delicious without it.

YIELD: 6 SERVINGS

CONTINUED

INGREDIENTS

Biscuits

- ▶ 1 cup (235 ml) unsweetened plant milk
- ▶ 1 tablespoon (15 ml) apple cider vinegar
- ▶ 2½ cups (300 g) self-rising flour, plus more for dusting
- ▶ 1 teaspoon sugar
- ▶ ½ teaspoon salt
- ▶ 1 teaspoon nutritional yeast
- ▶ ½ cup (112 g) vegan butter, frozen
- ▶ 2 tablespoons (28 ml) melted vegan butter

Gravy

- ▶ 1 cup (124 g) vegan ground sausage
- ▶ ¼ cup (55 g) vegan butter
- ▶ ¼ cup (32 g) all-purpose flour
- ▶ 2 cups (475 ml) unsweetened plant milk
- ▶ ½ teaspoon onion powder
- ▶ ½ teaspoon garlic powder
- ▶ ½ teaspoon mushroom seasoning
- ▶ Salt and pepper
- ▶ Dash of cayenne pepper

Assembly

- ▶ Chopped green onions or chives for garnish
- ▶ Cayenne pepper or smoked paprika for garnish

INSTRUCTIONS

Biscuits

1. Preheat the oven to 425°F (220°C or gas mark 7).

2. Combine the plant milk and apple cider vinegar in a small bowl, let it sit for 5 minutes to thicken for a vegan buttermilk. Meanwhile, add the flour, sugar, salt, and nutritional yeast to a large bowl and combine. Grate the frozen vegan butter into the dry ingredients, or use a pastry cutter or fork and break up the butter into pea-size pieces.

3. Make a well in the flour-butter mixture, then pour in the vegan buttermilk. Fold together with a wooden spoon until just mixed, being careful not to over work the dough. It will be quite shaggy. That's okay, it will come together with the next step!

4. Lay out the dough on a floured work surface and sprinkle a bit more flour onto the dough. With floured hands flatten it out, or rub some flour on a rolling pin and roll out the dough into a rectangle about ¾ to 1 inch (2 to 2.5 cm) thick. Fold the dough over itself like a letter for an envelope, so fold one-third over toward the center, then the other side over the rest of the dough. Gently flatten it by hand or rolling pin, turn it 90 degrees, and repeat that process four more times. Keep the flour handy in case the dough is still sticky.

5. Once the dough has been folded and flattened or rolled to ¾ inch (2 cm) thick, get a 3- or 3½-inch (7.5- or 9-cm) cookie cutter, lightly flour it, and cut out some biscuits. Don't twist the cookie cutter as this can prevent the biscuits from rising. Once all the available area has been cut out, take the scraps, reroll them, and cut out more biscuits. There should be six to eight depending on the size.

6. Add the biscuits to a parchment-lined baking sheet and make sure they are touching each other ever so slightly. This will help them rise as well! Throw them in the oven for 8 to 10 minutes, or until the tops start to brown. Pull them out and brush the tops with half of the melted vegan butter. Add them back into the oven for an additional 5 minutes, or until the tops are golden brown. Remove from the oven and brush with the rest of the melted vegan butter.

Gravy

1. Traditionally, this gravy is made with a roux using the fat from the sausage. However, all vegan sausages are not the same, and I recommend cooking the vegan sausage in a wide skillet over medium heat, then setting aside once it's nice and browned. Add the vegan butter and let it melt. Next, add the flour, 1 tablespoon (8 g) at a time, whisking between each tablespoon. Once the flour has been whisked in, let it cook off the raw flour taste for 1 minute or so, and add the plant milk, ½ cup (120 ml) at a time, and whisk in between.

2. Once all the milk has been whisked in, add the seasonings and the vegan sausage. Taste and adjust seasonings, and then simply reduce the gravy to the desired consistency.

Assembly

This couldn't be simpler! Pour a healthy portion of gravy over a split biscuit. Top with green onions, more cayenne pepper, or smoked paprika, and DIG IN!

CRACKER BARREL
HASH BROWN CASSEROLE

So, during my twenties, I played in bands. One of the reasons I did it was so I could tour, seeing the country and trying out all sorts of restaurants. When I say that, I mean everything from small local spots to chains I didn't have in my home state. I'd heard so many people rave about this place (perhaps ironically) and always wanted to try it. While I can't help you build the signature fireplace or ship you a checkers set or puzzle for your table, I can at least help you, make a copycat of this dish. If you like potatoes anywhere near as much as I do, perhaps you, too, will be eating this like a famished cartoon character—straight from the casserole dish!

YIELD: ABOUT 8 SERVINGS

INGREDIENTS

Soup

- 2 tablespoons (28 g) vegan butter
- 3 tablespoons (24 g) all-purpose flour
- ½ cup (120 ml) vegan chicken broth or veggie broth
- ¼ cup (60 ml) unsweetened plant milk
- ¼ teaspoon onion powder
- ¼ teaspoon garlic powder
- Salt and pepper

Casserole

- 2½ pounds (1.1 kg) frozen shredded potatoes
- ¼ cup (55 g) vegan butter, melted, plus more for the casserole dish
- 4 ounces (113 g) vegan sour cream, store-bought or homemade (page 86)
- 6 ounces (170 g) shredded vegan cheddar cheese, plus 4 ounces (113 g)
- ½ medium onion, diced
- 1 tablespoon (5 g) nutritional yeast
- 1 teaspoon garlic powder
- Salt and pepper

INSTRUCTIONS

Soup

Add the vegan butter to a medium saucepan or skillet over medium heat. Once melted, add the flour, 1 tablespoon (8 g) at a time, whisking between. When the flour has been incorporated, cook for 1 minute to get rid of the raw flour taste. Add the broth ¼ cup (60 ml) at a time, whisking between, followed by the plant milk. Add the seasonings, taste, and adjust accordingly. Bring to a simmer and reduce for 4 to 5 minutes, until slightly thickened. Remove from the heat.

Casserole

1. Preheat the oven to 350°F (175°C or gas mark 4). Mix all the ingredients including the soup in a large bowl (except 4 ounces [113 g] of vegan cheese for the topping). When thoroughly combined, grease a 9×13-inch (23×33-cm) casserole dish with vegan butter. Spread the hash brown mixture evenly, and then bake oven for 40 to 45 minutes.

2. Remove from the oven and then top with vegan cheese. Return to the oven for 10 minutes, then let it rest for at least 15 minutes. It will be scorching hot!

3. Serve as is or with some Southern Gravy Biscuits (page 129)!

MCDONALD'S HASH BROWNS

You'd think these would be vegan, but the originals are actually cooked in "natural beef flavor" and milk powder! The nerve! Fret not, these are easy to make at home. Getting them super crunchy on the outside while warm and fluffy on the inside is the key. They are perfect on their own with some ketchup or paired up with a McMuffin (page 120). Store these in the freezer and you can fry one up whenever you want, so they can be convenient, too.

YIELD: 5 TO 6 HASH BROWNS

INGREDIENTS

- 2 pounds (908 g) russet potatoes or frozen shredded potatoes
- Neutral oil for cooking
- 1 teaspoon salt
- 1 teaspoon black pepper
- ¼ teaspoon white pepper
- ½ teaspoon onion powder
- ½ teaspoon garlic powder
- ¼ cup (32 g) cornstarch
- Sea salt or flaky salt (optional)

INSTRUCTIONS

1. If using fresh potatoes, peel, wash, and grate the potatoes. Add them to a large bowl of cold water and let them soak for 10 to 15 minutes. Then, strain them and wrap them in a kitchen towel. Squeeze out as much water as possible. Add them to another towel and pat them dry.

2. Fill up a large pot or Dutch oven about halfway with a neutral oil (e.g., peanut, vegetable, or canola) and heat the oil to 210°F (99°C). It's important to keep the temperature between 200° and 220°F (93° and 104°C) so the potatoes don't get soggy or overcooked. Get the oil up to around 230°F (110°C) or so before adding as the temperature will most likely drop about 20 degrees. Just use a thermometer, keep an eye on it, and adjust the heat as needed.

3. Let the potatoes cook in the oil for 5 minutes, then remove with a slotted spoon and let them drain the excess oil. Once they are cool enough to handle, add the seasonings and cornstarch, and mix by hand.

4. Weigh out about 3½ ounces (100 g) of the mixture and roll it into a ball. Add the ball to a parchment-lined baking sheet. Using both hands, squish it and form it into an oblong hash brown patty, about ¾ inch (2 cm) thick.

5. Freeze the hash browns for at least 4 hours, or ideally overnight. Then, heat the oil up to 350° to 360°F (175° to 182°C). Fry them for 7 to 8 minutes, or until golden brown and beautiful. Let them rest on a wire rack, and season with some sea salt or flaky salt if desired. Serve as is or add them to a McMuffin (page 120)!

IHOP
NEW YORK CHEESECAKE
PANCAKES

Among the breakfast chains, this one was never my number one choice. But everyone has their favorites, so due to friends and family I ate here plenty. And, when I did, I always got the most ridiculous special I could order. This seems like it would make it to the top of that list! We'll be making a delicious strawberry topping (use the leftovers in a Blizzard, page 168). And we'll take some of our delicious Cheesecake (page 149), chop it up, and bake it inside the pancakes! The cheesecake melts and creates these ooey gooey pockets of tangy sweetness that are just absurdly good, especially when paired with the strawberry compote topping!

**YIELD: 4 LARGE PANCAKES
(PLUS EXTRA TOPPING)**

INGREDIENTS

Strawberry Topping

- 1 pound (454 g) fresh or frozen strawberries
- ½ cup (100 g) sugar
- 2 teaspoons (10 ml) lemon juice
- 1 tablespoon (8 g) cornstarch plus 2 tablespoons (28 ml) water
- 2 tablespoons (16 g) confectioners' sugar

Pancakes

- 1 cup (175 g) diced vegan cheesecake, store-bought or homemade (page 149)
- 1¼ cups (295 ml) unsweetened plant milk plus 1 tablespoon (15 ml) apple cider vinegar
- 1½ cups (180 g) all-purpose flour
- 1 tablespoon (14 g) baking powder
- 3 tablespoons (39 g) sugar
- ½ teaspoon salt
- 1 teaspoon vanilla extract
- 2 tablespoons (28 ml) vegetable or refined coconut oil
- Nonstick cooking spray
- Vegan whipped cream for topping

INSTRUCTIONS

Strawberry Topping

1. Roughly chop the strawberries and add them along with the sugar and lemon juice to a medium saucepan over medium heat.Bring to a simmer and continue to cook for 2 to 3 minutes, or until they have released about ½ cup (120 ml) of juice.

2. Combine the cornstarch and water, then add the cornstarch slurry and confectioners' sugar to the strawberry mixture. This should thicken the sauce, but you can add more of each for an even thicker sauce. Remove from the heat and reserve.

Pancakes

1. Dice up the frozen cheesecake and then return it to the freezer in a small bowl. Combine the plant milk and vinegar in a bowl and let rest to thicken for 10-30 minutes. The longer it rests, the fluffier the pancakes will be!

2. Add the flour, baking powder, sugar, and salt to a large bowl and combine thoroughly. Then, add the vanilla and oil to the milk and vinegar mixture and whisk to incorporate. Dump the wet mixture into the flour mixture. Fold until just combined and there are no dry flour spots visible.

3. Bring a nonstick skillet or griddle up to medium heat and spray with some cooking spray. Pour in about ½ cup (120 ml) of the pancake batter. Drop a few pieces of the diced frozen cheesecake onto the pancake and gently press them in to submerge. Add more batter to cover as needed as the cheesecake will burn if it comes into direct contact with the pan.

4. After 3 minutes or so, check the pancake and flip once it's golden brown.

5. Stack the pancakes on a plate, top with the strawberry topping and some vegan whipped cream, and enjoy!

BURGER KING FRENCH TOAST STICKS

This is one of the rare items that is actually plant-based, so I just went down the street and picked some up. I gotta say, the ones I had were on the bland side and not very sweet, which is weird for a fast-food place! We can definitely do better. And these will be ready in less time than it takes to go to the drive-through. (Well maybe not quite, but they are so much better you won't care!) The outside is crunchy and sweet from the cinnamon sugar, and the inside is soft and fluffy. It's like if a churro and French toast had a baby!

YIELD: 2 TO 4 SERVINGS

INGREDIENTS

French Toast
- 6 slices Texas toast or any thick-sliced bread
- Neutral oil for cooking
- Maple syrup for dipping

Wet Dredge
- 1 tablespoon (14 g) ground flax plus 3 tablespoons (45 ml) water (or 1 vegan egg replacement of choice)
- ½ cup (120 ml) unsweetened plant milk
- ⅛ teaspoon ground cinnamon
- Pinch of ground nutmeg
- Pinch of allspice

Dry Dredge
- ¼ cup (32 g) all-purpose flour
- 1 tablespoon (8 g) cornstarch

Cinnamon Sugar
- ⅓ cup (66 g) sugar
- 1 teaspoon ground cinnamon

INSTRUCTIONS

French Toast

1. Cut each slice of bread into three sticks. Don't worry about taking the crust off.

2. Mix the flax egg by combining the ground flax and water. Then, prepare the dredging station by adding the ingredients for the wet dredge and the dry dredge in two shallow bowls.

3. Heat up 3 tablespoons (45 ml) of neutral oil in a 12-inch (30-cm) skillet over medium heat. Once the oil is hot, dredge the sticks in the dry dredge, coating thoroughly. Then, coat them in the wet dredge. Carefully add them to the oil. The wet dredge may cause the oil to sputter for a few seconds. Don't be alarmed; it will calm down.

4. Fry each stick on each side until golden brown and crispy, and just begging to be eaten, but resist that urge.

Cinnamon Sugar

Combine the cinnamon and sugar in a bowl. Thoroughly coat the French toast sticks in the cinnamon sugar. Let cool for a couple minutes, then dip in some maple syrup and enjoy!

WAFFLE HOUSE APPLE CINNAMON WAFFLE

One of my good friends told me people only go to Waffle House after a night of drinking . . . and even then, partly because it's cheap. That was news to me. Having lived in California most of my life, I just didn't know its reputation, I guess! I find the menu there pretty straightforward and almost boring except for this item from their secret menu. While it's one of the more obscure items in this book, I think you'll find it makes a super delicious and decadent breakfast . . . or you know, a 2 a.m. treat. (Just make it ahead of time, so you can reheat it instead of cooking it when the time comes!)

YIELD: 5 TO 6 WAFFLES

INGREDIENTS

Apple Topping

- ▶ 2 tablespoons (28 g) vegan butter
- ▶ 4 Granny Smith apples, peeled and diced
- ▶ 2 tablespoons (26 g) sugar
- ▶ ¼ cup (60 g) packed brown sugar
- ▶ 1 teaspoon ground cinnamon
- ▶ ⅛ teaspoon ground nutmeg
- ▶ ⅛ teaspoon ground allspice
- ▶ Pinch of garam masala
- ▶ ¼ teaspoon salt
- ▶ 2 teaspoons (10 ml) lemon juice
- ▶ ½ tablespoon (4 g) cornstarch
- ▶ 1 tablespoon (15 ml) water

Waffles

- ▶ 1½ cups (355 ml) unsweetened plant milk
- ▶ 1½ tablespoons (25 ml) apple cider vinegar
- ▶ 2 cups (240 g) all-purpose flour
- ▶ 1½ tablespoons (21 g) baking powder
- ▶ 3 tablespoons (39 g) granulated sugar
- ▶ 3 tablespoons (45 g) packed brown granulated sugar
- ▶ 1 teaspoon salt
- ▶ 1 teaspoon vanilla extract
- ▶ 5 tablespoons (70 g) unsalted vegan butter, melted
- ▶ Vegan whipped cream for serving (optional)

INSTRUCTIONS

Apple Topping

1. Melt the vegan butter in a saucepan over medium heat. Add the apples and stir to coat in the butter. Cook down for 3 minutes, or until the apples start to soften. Add the rest of the ingredients except the cornstarch and water and stir to combine. Cook for 8 minutes, or until the apples are soft, but still have a bit of bite to them; they should not be mushy or close to it.

2. Combine the cornstarch and water in a small bowl, and then add it to the saucepan and stir. Add more to thicken the sauce even more. Remove from the heat.

Waffles

1. Combine the plant milk and apple cider vinegar. Let it sit for 15 minutes to form a vegan buttermilk. In the meantime, combine the flour, baking powder, granulated sugar and brown sugar, and salt in a large bowl. Pour in the vegan buttermilk, vanilla, and melted vegan butter. Stir to combine, just until there are no dry flour spots left. Let the batter rest for 15 minutes.

2. Heat up a waffle iron. Then add ½ to ⅔ cup (120 to 160 ml) of the waffle batter and cook until it's as golden brown as you like. Top with plenty of the apples, and maybe some vegan whipped cream if you like!

NOTE: Waffles can be frozen and enjoyed later. Just pop them in an oven preheated to 400°F (200°C) for 6 to 8 minutes. They will actually get a little crispier, too!

STARBUCKS PUMPKIN CREAM CHEESE MUFFINS

So, I definitely worked multiple jobs within walking distance of one of these places—which makes sense seeing as they are on every street corner in the country. I most often ordered a breakfast sandwich when I was getting something to eat in my pre-vegan days. But there's no denying the appeal of this super delicious and decadent pumpkin-spiced muffin with a cream cheese filling! What I love about this recipe is these muffins are good for a few days, so you can whip them up and have an easy and quick breakfast all week—and with no dairy and no waiting in line like a chump!

YIELD: 12 MUFFINS

NOTE: If you want extra big muffin tops, aim for more like 10 muffins.

INGREDIENTS

Cream Cheese Filling

- 8 ounces (226 g) vegan cream cheese, softened
- ½ cup (100 g) sugar
- 1 teaspoon vanilla extract

Muffins

- 2 tablespoons (28 g) ground flax plus 5 tablespoons (73 ml) water
- 2 cups (250 g) all-purpose flour
- ½ teaspoon salt
- 1 teaspoon baking powder
- 1 teaspoon baking soda
- 1 tablespoon (6 g) pumpkin pie spice
- ½ cup (100 g) granulated sugar
- ½ cup (115 g) packed brown sugar
- 1 can (15 ounces, or 425 g) pumpkin puree
- ½ cup (112 g) vegan butter, melted
- Nonstick cooking spray
- ⅓ cup (43 g) dry-roasted pumpkin seeds, roughly chopped

INSTRUCTIONS

Cream Cheese Filling

Add the softened cream cheese to a medium bowl with the sugar and vanilla. Whisk, or ideally use a hand mixer, to whip the mixture together until creamy and smooth. Add the filling to a tipped piping bag or a zip-top bag.

Muffins

1. Preheat the oven to 375°F (190°C).

2. Combine the flax and water in a small bowl. Set aside for 5 minutes to thicken.

3. In a large bowl, combine the flour, salt, baking powder, baking soda, pumpkin spice, granulated sugar, and brown sugar. In another bowl, combine the pumpkin puree, flax egg mixture, and melted vegan butter. Gently fold the wet ingredients into the dry ingredients; stop once there is no more dry flour visible.

4. Line a 12-cup muffin tin with paper liners, and lightly spray them with cooking spray. Fill each muffin liner about three-quarters of the way for regular-size muffins or fill them up all the way for bigger muffins with a bigger muffin top.

5. Gently insert the tipped piping bag or zip-top bag into the top center of each muffin and squeeze out 2 to 3 tablespoons (28 to 45 ml) of the filling into each muffin. Sprinkle on 1 tablespoon (4 g) of the roasted pumpkin seeds.

NOTE: If using raw pumpkin seeds, roast them in a dry skillet for 4 minutes, or until they brown a little and become aromatic.

6. Bake for 15 to 20 minutes. Test the doneness with a toothpick by inserting it into the center of the muffin (through the side of the muffin to avoid the cream cheese top). If it comes out clean with no runny batter, the muffins are done! Remove from the oven and allow to cool, then enjoy with a cup of homemade coffee!

DESSERTS

CHAPTER 6

KRISPY KREME DOUGHNUTS
146

WHITE CASTLE CHEESECAKE ON A STICK
149

MCDONALD'S APPLE PIE
152

CINNABON CLASSIC ROLL
155

SONIC CHERRY LIMEADE
158

TACO BELL CINNABON® DELIGHTS
160

BOB'S BIG BOY BOB'S® FAMOUS HOT FUDGE CAKE
163

WENDY'S FROSTY®
166

DAIRY QUEEN OREO® BLIZZARD®
168

CHICK-FIL-A PEACH MILKSHAKE
170

KRISPY KREME DOUGHNUTS

I remember when this chain came to Southern California in the late '90s. A few friends and I trekked out to Orange County (which was about two hours from where we lived) just to get in a one-hour drive-thru wait. Eating those fresh, hot doughnuts at 1 a.m. in a parking lot is one of my favorite food memories! These doughnuts are just as good as the non-vegan version, and have a light, fluffy interior. The key is absolutely drenching them in the signature glaze, so they are crispy and creamy at the same time!

YIELD: ABOUT 24 DOUGHNUTS

INGREDIENTS

Yeast Mixture

- 2½ teaspoons (8 g) instant yeast
- ¼ cup (60 ml) water, heated to 110° to 120°F (43° to 49°C)
- ½ teaspoon sugar

Dough

- 4½ cups (540 g) all-purpose flour, divided, plus more for working the dough
- ½ cup (100 g) sugar
- 1 teaspoon salt
- 1 teaspoon ground nutmeg
- 1 teaspoon vanilla extract
- 2 vegan egg replacements (page 27)
- 1½ cups (355 ml) unsweetened plant milk
- ½ cup (100 g) shortening, plus more for working the dough

Glaze

- 2½ cups (300 g) confectioners' sugar
- ¼ cup (60 ml) unsweetened plant milk, plus more if needed
- 3 tablespoons (45 ml) light corn syrup

Frying

- Neutral oil for cooking

INSTRUCTIONS

Yeast Mixture

Add the ingredients to a 1-cup (235-ml) measuring cup. Let it get foamy and rise for 10 minutes.

Dough

1. In the bowl of a stand mixer, add 2¼ cups (270 g) of flour, plus everything else except the shortening. Mix on medium speed for 3 minutes. Add the rest of the flour and mix for 3 minutes. Last, add the shortening, mixing for a final 3 minutes.

2. This dough will be fairly wet and sticky, so lightly grease a cutting board and a large bowl. Working with lightly greased hands, dump the dough ball out onto the work surface. Knead it for 1 to 2 minutes and form it into a ball. Then, add it to the greased bowl and cover with plastic wrap. Let the dough proof and rise for at least 90 minutes, or until doubled in size.

3. Once risen, punch it down and degas it. Luckily it will be much less sticky at this point, but flour the work surface and a rolling pin. Next, roll the dough ball into a rectangle shape about ½ inch (1 cm) thick.

4. Cut out doughnut shapes with a cookie cutter, using a large one for the doughnut and a smaller one for the doughnut hole. Reroll the scraps and cut out as many doughnuts as possible. Let the doughnuts rest on a parchment-lined baking sheet.

CONTINUED

INSTRUCTIONS

Glaze

Whisk or mix with a hand mixer to combine all the ingredients, adding more plant milk for a thinner glaze. Set aside.

Frying

1. Bring a large pot of neutral oil to 330° to 340°F (167° to 171°C), this is the perfect temperature so try to keep it in this zone. Too low and the doughnuts will come out oily, too high and they'll get way to dark and crunchy on the outside.

2. Once the oil is up to temperature, carefully add two or three doughnuts at a time. If the doughnuts are hard to pick up without stretching, cut the parchment paper around them, and then turn upside down and let gravity slowly detach the doughnut from the parchment paper into the oil. Be careful doing this, but I've found it to be much easier than simply dropping the doughnuts in with bare hands.

3. Fry for 90 seconds, or until lightly golden brown, then flip and fry for 90 seconds. Let them rest on a wire rack.

4. Once the doughnuts are cool enough to handle but still warm, dunk them in the glaze. A fork is recommended to lift and flip them as this will allow the glaze to drip off.

5. Once coated thoroughly, let them rest on a wire rack until the glaze has hardened, then dig in!

WHITE CASTLE CHEESECAKE ON A STICK

Originally, I was going to do a cheesecake from the Cheesecake Factory in this book, but when I was doing research, I came across this amazing creation and knew I had to make it! This is actually a no-bake cheesecake recipe, so the filling is a bit softer than traditional cheesecake. But I think you'll find it's just as delicious and decadent as any baked cheesecake recipe. You can obviously eat it as a regular cheesecake and skip the chocolate magic shell, but I highly recommend dipping it and eating it on a stick! It's way more fun and unique and is just way better than some boring old cheesecake on a plate. And if you are going to eat it like normal cheesecake, why not top it with the strawberry topping from the New York Cheesecake Pancakes (page 136).

YIELD: 8 SERVINGS

CONTINUED

INGREDIENTS

Crust

- ▶ 9 ounces (250 g) vegan graham crackers, or crackers/cookies of choice
- ▶ ½ cup (112 g) vegan butter, melted
- ▶ Nonstick cooking spray

Cheesecake Filling

- ▶ 3 cups (420 g) raw cashews
- ▶ Boiling water for soaking
- ▶ Scant 1½ cups (350 g) coconut cream
- ▶ 2 teaspoons (6 g) lactic acid
- ▶ 1 teaspoon salt
- ▶ ¼ cup (60 g) vegan sour cream, store-bought or homemade (page 86)
- ▶ ½ cup (100 g) sugar
- ▶ 2 teaspoons (10 ml) vanilla extract
- ▶ ½ cup (50 g) confectioners' sugar
- ▶ Nonstick cooking spray

Magic Shell

- ▶ 10 ounces (283 g) vegan chocolate chips
- ▶ ¼ cup (54 g) refined coconut oil

INSTRUCTIONS

Crust

1. Preheat the oven to 350°F (175°C or gas mark 4).

2. To make the crust, crush up the cookies in a food processor. Alternatively, use a blender; this might have to be done in batches. Or just put them in a bag and pound them with a rolling pin. Combine the crushed cookies with the melted vegan butter. Stir until well combined. The mixture should be able to clump together easily.

3. Get a 9-inch (23-cm) springform pan and grease it with cooking spray or cut out a circle of parchment paper and line the bottom of the pan with that. (You can use an 8-inch [20-cm] or 10-inch [26-cm] pan, but the filling will be a little taller or shorter.)

4. Add the cookie mixture to the pan and using something with a flat bottom (like a glass) lightly press down and even out the crust. Bake for 10 minutes, then remove from the oven and set aside.

Cheesecake Filling

1. Soak the cashews in boiling water for 10 to 15 minutes. Then, add everything to a blender. For the coconut cream, only use the cream, reserve the coconut water at the bottom for another recipe. Blend at high speed until smooth and no bits of cashews remain.

2. Grease the sides of the springform pan with some cooking spray, then pour in the filling. Wrap the top with plastic wrap and then heavy-duty aluminum foil and freeze for 6 hours or overnight.

3. Remove the sides of the springform pan and let the cheesecake thaw for 10 to 15 minutes on the countertop. Once soft enough, slice into eight equal pieces.

4. Stick an ice pop stick into each slice. Return the cheesecake slices to the freezer on top of a parchment-lined baking sheet for 20 to 30 minutes, or until fairly frozen.

Magic Shell

1. To make the magic shell, melt the chocolate and coconut oil in a double boiler. Get a medium-size saucepan and fill it with about 1 inch (2.5 cm) of water. Place a heatproof bowl on top; it should be big enough that it doesn't touch the water, but small enough that it dips into the saucepan. Add the chocolate and coconut oil, then heat over medium-low and stir the chocolate and coconut oil until completely melted. If it seems like the mixture is melting too quickly, kill the heat and continue to stir. Once everything is melted completely, fill a measuring cup with the chocolate magic shell.

2. Dip each piece of cheesecake into the magic shell, let the excess drip off, then place on the parchment-lined baking sheet which should still be cold from the freezer. This will help the bottom of the chocolate set and firm up. The magic shell will become hard within a minute or two. Once this happens, dig in and enjoy!

3. You can use some of the Cheesecake in the New York Cheesecake Pancakes recipe on page 136!

MCDONALD'S APPLE PIE

Alright, the story on these goes that they used to be deep-fried up until the early 1990s. Then, I guess there was some concern about how unhealthy they were, so they baked them. My question is, of all the things to be concerned with at this place it's the fried apple pie? In any case, for years, people in the know have been pining for the days of the fried pie. Well, I tried it both ways, and I was shocked to learn that I actually prefer the baked! That being said, if you want to try this recipe fried, be my guest!

YIELD: 8 PIES

INGREDIENTS

Apple Filling
- 2 tablespoons (28 g) vegan butter
- 4 Granny Smith apples, peeled and diced
- 2 tablespoons (26 g) sugar
- ¼ cup (60 g) packed brown sugar
- 1 teaspoon ground cinnamon
- ⅛ teaspoon ground nutmeg
- ⅛ teaspoon allspice
- Pinch of garam masala
- ¼ teaspoon salt
- 2 teaspoons (10 ml) lemon juice
- ½ tablespoon (4 g) cornstarch, plus more as needed
- 1 tablespoon (15 ml) water, plus more as needed

Cinnamon Sugar
- ¼ cup (50 g) sugar
- 1 tablespoon (7 g) ground cinnamon

Puff Pastry
- 1 package (17.3 ounces, or 490 g) vegan puff pastry
- 2 tablespoons (28 g) vegan butter, melted

INSTRUCTIONS

Apple Pie Filling

1. Melt the vegan butter in a saucepan over medium heat. Add the apples and stir to coat in the butter. Cook down for 3 minutes, or until the apples start to soften. Add the rest of the ingredients, except the cornstarch and water. Stir to combine, then cook for 8 minutes or so, or until the apples are soft but still have a bit of bite to them. They should not be mushy or close to it.

2. Combine the cornstarch and water in a small bowl. Add it to the saucepan and stir. Add more to thicken the sauce even more. Remove from the heat.

Cinnamon Sugar

1. In a small bowl, stir together the sugar and cinnamon until evenly distributed. Set aside.

CONTINUED

Puff Pastry

1. Preheat the oven to 400°F (205°C or gas mark 6).

2. Roll out the puff pastry so it's a 10×10-inch (26×26-cm) square. Cut it in half, then into thirds; you should end up with eight pieces that are 5 inches by 2½ inches (13 by 6 cm). Add some apple pie filling to one piece of puff pastry, about 2 to 3 tablespoons (25 to 35 g) to the middle. Leave plenty of space around the edges, so the filling doesn't escape out the sides.

3. Brush the edges with some melted vegan butter or vegan milk, then take another piece of puff pastry and add it on top. Seal the edges by hand, then crimp them with a fork. Cut three to four slits into the pie to let steam escape. Add to a parchment-lined baking sheet. Repeat with the rest of the puff pastry.

4. Once all the pies have been formed, brush them each with some melted vegan butter and sprinkle on some of the cinnamon sugar. Bake them for 25 to 30 minutes, checking around the halfway point and rotating the baking sheet if they are cooking unevenly. Keep an eye on them as they can go from beautifully browned to blackened and burnt in no time.

5. When they are done, let them rest for a few minutes. (I know it's tempting to go for them right away, but a burnt roof of the mouth is never fun.) When they are cool enough, go ahead and dig in!

DEEP-FRIED PIE

To deep fry these, simply skip cutting the slits or adding the brushed vegan butter and cinnamon sugar. Then fry them at 350°F (175°C or gas mark 4) until golden brown. Let them rest on a wire rack for 30 seconds, then immediately toss them in cinnamon sugar, and there you go you got a fried pie!

CINNABON CLASSIC ROLL

I honestly haven't had this sweet treat since the '90s when I was a disaffected teenage punk. I remember thinking that they sounded like a good idea, but every time I got one, I could barely make it halfway through before the sugar and grease was just too much. It just kind of made me sad, which is the opposite of what a cinnamon roll should do. Then again, maybe it was the teenage angst! Either way, my wife took these to work the day after I made them and her non-vegan coworkers said they were better than Cinnabon, so maybe my teenage punk self was right.

YIELD: 8 TO 10 ROLLS

NOTE: These are standard-size rolls as shown in the photos, not the over the top XXL size served at the restaurant. Feel free to scale up if you think you can handle it!

CONTINUED

INGREDIENTS

Dough

- ▶ 1½ tablespoons (21 g) ground flax plus 3 tablespoons (45 ml) water
- ▶ 1 cup (235 ml) unsweetened plant milk, heated to 110°F (43°C)
- ▶ ¼ cup (55 g) vegan butter, melted
- ▶ 2¼ teaspoons (7 g) instant yeast
- ▶ ¼ cup (50 g) sugar
- ▶ 1 teaspoon salt
- ▶ 4 cups (480 g) bread flour, plus more as needed
- ▶ Neutral oil for preparing the bowl

Filling

- ▶ 1 cup (225 g) packed brown sugar
- ▶ 2 tablespoons (14 g) ground cinnamon
- ▶ ¼ teaspoon allspice
- ▶ ¼ cup (55 g) vegan butter, softened

Icing

- ▶ 4 ounces (113 g) vegan cream cheese, softened
- ▶ 2 tablespoons (28 ml) unsweetened plant milk
- ▶ 1 teaspoon vanilla extract
- ▶ 3 tablespoons (42 g) vegan butter, softened
- ▶ 1 cup (120 g) confectioners' sugar

INSTRUCTIONS

Dough

1. To make the flax egg, combine the ground flax and water in a small bowl. Let it sit and thicken for 5 minutes. Then, in the bowl of a stand mixer, combine all the dough ingredients except the flour. Mix until combined, then add the flour and fold in with a spatula.

2. Attach the dough hook to the stand mixer. Knead the dough on medium speed for 8 minutes. If the dough is too sticky, add 1 tablespoon (8 g) of flour until it pulls away from the bowl. Grease another bowl with oil, then add the dough ball to it and cover with a towel or plastic wrap. Allow the dough to rise for 1 to 2 hours, or until doubled in size.

3. Gently deflate the dough. Dust a work surface with flour, then roll the dough out on it into a rectangle about 16×10 inches (41×26 cm).

Filling

Combine the brown sugar, cinnamon, and allspice in a small bowl. Spread the softened butter all over the rolled-out dough, leaving a ½-inch (1-cm) margin around the border. Sprinkle on the cinnamon sugar mixture and spread evenly. Gently press it into the dough. It will seem like a lot, but that will give us an ooey gooey cinnamon roll with a caramelized bottom!

Rolls

1. Starting at the bottom of the widest section (the 16-inch [41-cm] section) roll the dough over itself. Go along the entire length of the fold and tightly tuck it in. Once the initial roll feels tight and sealed, continue to roll it over itself again, trying to keep it as tight as possible. Once the dough has been rolled about halfway it will get much easier. Roll it all the way and tuck the seam side down.

2. Cut off the very ends of the roll as these will not have that much filling in them. Using a serrated knife or ideally kitchen twine or unflavored floss (cinnamon flavored might be okay!) cut out sections 2 inches (5 cm) wide. Add each roll to greased 9×13-inch (23×33-cm) pan, leaving about 1 or 2 inches (2.5 to 5 cm) of space between each roll. Once all rolls have been cut and added to the pan, cover with plastic wrap and let them proof for 30 minutes.

3. Preheat the oven to 350°F (175°C or gas mark 4) and then take the plastic wrap off the pan. Bake for 25 to 30 minutes, or until the rolls are slightly golden brown on top.

Icing

1. While the rolls are baking, make the icing. Combine all the icing ingredients in a medium bowl and mix with a hand mixer or whisk until smooth and creamy!

2. Once the rolls are done baking, let them rest for 5 minutes, then drizzle on the icing with abandon! Let the rolls cool for 5 minutes and then serve immediately! These are best fresh, but like I said, my wife took the leftovers to work the next day and her coworkers said they were better than Cinnabon, so they are still pretty good cold. You can heat them up in the microwave for 20 to 30 seconds, too.

SONIC CHERRY LIMEADE

Okay, sure, I didn't have to veganize it. But this is hands down my favorite soda-based drink of all time! It's quite simple to make, and the best part is that you can tailor this to your taste—add as much or as little of the cherry lime syrup as you'd like. Store the mixture in the fridge and add it to soda as you like; this way you can always have a fresh one whenever. If you add all of the cherry lime to a larger container of soda, make sure you drink it before it all goes flat— hence why I like to mix it when needed!

YIELD: 12 SERVINGS

INGREDIENTS

Simple Syrup
- 1 cup (200 g) sugar
- 1 cup (235 ml) lime juice

Assembly
- 2 jars (10 ounces, or 283 g each) maraschino cherries
- Lemon-lime soda, such as 7 Up® or Sprite®
- Lime slices

INSTRUCTIONS

Simple Syrup

1. To make this, combine the sugar and lime juice in a small saucepan. Heat over medium heat, until the sugar has completely melted and the resulting mixture is smooth. It will be quite sweet and sour!

2. Combine the simple syrup with the cherry syrup from the two jars of maraschino cherries (reserve the cherries for serving). This liquid can be stored in the fridge and used as needed.

Assembly

1. Mix 3 to 4 tablespoons (45 to 60 ml) of the cherry lime simple syrup with 12 ounces (354 ml) of lemon-lime soda. Garnish with a lime and some cherries.

2. Enjoy over ice with some Chili Cheese Tots (page 100) or Onion Rings (page 110) for the full experience. Add more of the cherry lime simple syrup per can of soda to preference!

TACO BELL CINNABON® DELIGHTS

A lot of folks like the twists at this chain, and I don't blame them. But for me, these were always my go-to! I mean, it's a donut hole with cream cheese filling and cinnamon sugar . . . why choose anything else? Pair them with a Crunchwrap (page 66) or a Mexican Pizza (page 70) for a complete dinner and dessert experience!

YIELD: 16 PIECES

> **NOTE:** To make yeast donut holes, just make a half recipe of the Krispy Kreme Doughnuts (page 146).

INGREDIENTS

Cream Filling
- ¼ cup (60 g) vegan cream cheese, softened
- 2 tablespoons (28 g) vegan butter, softened
- 1 cup (120 g) confectioners' sugar
- 1 teaspoon vanilla extract

Cinnamon Sugar
- ½ cup (100 g) sugar
- 1 tablespoon (7 g) ground cinnamon

Dough
- 2 cups (240 g) all-purpose flour
- ¼ cup (50 g) sugar
- 2 teaspoons (5 g) ground cinnamon
- ¼ teaspoon allspice
- 1 tablespoon (14 g) baking powder
- 1 teaspoon salt
- 1 tablespoon (14 g) ground flax plus 2 tablespoons (28 ml) water
- ½ cup (120 ml) unsweetened plant milk
- 3 tablespoons (42 g) vegan butter, melted
- Neutral oil for cooking

INSTRUCTIONS

Cream Filling

Let the vegan cream cheese and butter rest until it's at room temperature and softened. Add them to a medium bowl with the rest of the ingredients and mix with a whisk or hand blender. Add the filling to a piping bag with a tip. Set aside.

Cinnamon Sugar

Combine the sugar and cinnamon in a large bowl (big enough to toss the donut holes in).

Dough

1. Combine the flour, sugar, cinnamon, allspice, baking powder, and salt in a large bowl. Combine the ground flax and water in a small bowl and let it sit and thicken for 5 minutes, then combine it with the plant milk and vegan butter. Pour the wet mixture into the dry mixture, and fold until just combined and no dry flour is visible.

2. Fill a large pot or Dutch oven about halfway with a neutral oil (e.g., peanut, vegetable, or canola) and heat to 350° to 360°F (175° to 182°C). Using wet hands, roll about 2 tablespoons of the donut batter into a ball. Fry these in batches and avoid crowding the pot. Carefully drop them into the oil. Fry for 3 minutes, turning every 30 seconds or so to ensure that the entire donut hole gets fried. When they are golden brown, let them rest on a wire rack for 10 seconds and then toss in the cinnamon sugar mixture until fully coated.

3. Once they have all been fried and cooled, firmly insert the tip of the piping bag into the center and fill with 1 to 2 tablespoons (10 to 20 g) of the filling. Serve and eat immediately and enjoy!

HOW TO MAKE VEGAN ICE CREAM

There are lots of different ways to make vegan ice cream, all with different pros and cons. The recipes in this book are no-churn simply because I, like many other folks, don't have an ice cream machine. But I've found that with a few tricks, you can make something just as decadent and rich as any churned ice cream, dairy or not.

This is a basic vanilla ice cream recipe and can be modified as you see fit. The base will be full-fat coconut milk. I've experimented with coconut cream, and I found that to be a bit too rich. In order for the milk to separate from the water, you'll need to chill it in your fridge for about 24 hours. After that it's really just a matter of whipping it and then blending it with some sugar and whatever flavoring you wish.

For blending, I've tried out a stand mixer, a hand mixer, and a high-speed blender. Both the hand and stand mixers take longer, but you're less likely to over blend, which can cause the coconut milk to curdle and separate. Blending in a high-speed blender is much faster and efficient, but the risk of over-blending is obviously much higher! I suggest if you are going to use a high-speed blender that you do so just until everything is combined and then stop immediately. This is my preferred method, but it did take a few tries to get it right.

For the sugar, you can use agave or a combination of agave and regular sugar. Maple syrup can also be used, but make sure it's an ice cream flavor that will go well with it. I once tried making mint-chip ice cream with maple syrup. The mint and maple did not pair particularly well.

YIELD: 4 SERVINGS

INGREDIENTS

▶ 2 cans (13.5 ounces, or 400 ml each) full fat coconut milk (chilled for 24 hours)

▶ ⅔ cup (160 ml) agave syrup (or ⅓ cup agave [80 ml] and ⅓ cup [67 g] sugar)

▶ 1 tablespoon (15 ml) vanilla extract

1. Scoop out the hardened coconut cream at the top of the coconut milk cans and place into a high-speed blender. Discard or reserve the coconut water in the can for another use. Blend the coconut cream with the agave (and sugar, if using) and until just combined.

2. Alternatively, chill a bowl and the beaters of a hand mixer or stand mixer in the freezer for 10 minutes. Then, mix the coconut milk with a hand mixer or stand mixer. If the coconut milk is too stiff to blend, add 1 tablespoon (15 ml) of the coconut water to loosen it up. After about 5 minutes it should be whipped and forming stiff peaks just like whipped cream. Add about half of the agave and blend to combine, then add the last half and repeat. Lastly, add the vanilla extract and blend.

3. Pour the mixture into a freezer-friendly container, such as a metal loaf pan, and cover with foil. Freeze it for at least 6 hours or overnight. If mix-ins are desired, simply stir them in after it's been freezing for 2 hours, freeze for another 4 hours to overnight, and enjoy the next day!

BOB'S BIG BOY
BOB'S FAMOUS
HOT FUDGE CAKE

Okay, this one was a big deal for me as a kid. I used to go to the original location in Burbank, California, with my family and every time I'd beg to get one of these. My parents would tell me that if I finished my Big Boy (a double-decker burger that preceded the Big Mac by almost thirty years) that I could order dessert. Well, that was a beast of a burger, especially for my ten-year-old stomach! But there were a handful of times that I bested that beast and was able to enjoy all of three or four bites of this cake before I was just too full to eat anymore! And for good reason, this thing is super fudgy, rich, and decadent! Even as a grown-up, I can't eat an entire one of these, so sharing is recommended.

YIELD: 4 VERY LARGE SERVINGS OR 8 REGULAR SERVINGS

NOTE: To make a double-decker cake like the photo, it's necessary to double this ice cream recipe.

CONTINUED

INGREDIENTS

Hot Fudge

- 1 can (13.5 ounces, or 400 ml) full-fat coconut milk
- 2 tablespoons (28 g) vegan butter
- ¼ cup (60 g) packed brown sugar
- ¼ cup (60 ml) corn syrup or maple syrup
- 2 teaspoons (10 ml) vanilla extract
- ¼ teaspoon salt
- ½ cup (40 g) unsweetened cocoa powder, sifted
- 6 ounces (170 g) dark chocolate chips

Vanilla Ice Cream

- 2 cans (13.5 ounces, or 400 ml) coconut milk (chilled)
- ⅔ cup (230 g) maple syrup
- 1 tablespoon (15 ml) vanilla extract
- Pinch of ground cinnamon
- Pinch of ground nutmeg
- Pinch of salt
- 1 tablespoon (15 ml) bourbon (optional)

Cake

- 1¼ cups (150 g) all-purpose flour
- 1 cup (200 g) sugar
- 1 teaspoon baking soda
- ½ teaspoon salt
- ½ cup (40 g) unsweetened cocoa powder, sifted
- ½ cup (120 ml) unsweetened plant milk plus ½ tablespoon (8 ml) apple cider vinegar
- ½ cup (120 ml) hot strong coffee
- ¼ cup (60 ml) vegetable oil
- 1 teaspoon vanilla extract
- Nonstick cooking spray

Assembly

- Vegan whipped cream for topping
- Cherries for topping

INSTRUCTIONS

Hot Fudge

1. Add everything except the cocoa powder and chocolate chips to a medium saucepan over medium-low heat and whisk frequently. Bring to a simmer and once everything has been whisked together and is emulsified, add the cocoa powder and whisk to incorporate. Next add the chocolate chips and continue whisking until melted.

2. The fudge will be thin so reduce it down over medium-low heat, whisking frequently, for 5 to 7 minutes, or until desired thickness. Keep in mind it will thicken more as it cools. Store in a heatproof container in the fridge until needed.

Vanilla Ice Cream

Chill the coconut milk in the top shelf of the refrigerator overnight. Only use the cream from the coconut milk, reserving the water for a smoothie or something else. Then, add all the ingredients to a high-speed blender and blend until thoroughly combined, using a tamper as needed. Blend just until everything is combined, making sure not to over blend as this can cause the cream to separate and curdle. Add to a freezer safe container (a bread loaf pan works) and cover. Freeze overnight. The next day it should be nice and creamy!

Cake

1. Preheat the oven to 350°F (175°C or gas mark 4). Combine the flour, sugar, baking soda, salt, and sifted cocoa powder in a large bowl. In a small bowl, add the plant milk and apple cider vinegar and let it rest to curdle for 5 minutes. Next, combine the coffee, oil, vanilla, and vegan buttermilk mixture in another bowl. Dump the wet ingredients into the dry flour mixture. Mix by hand or with a hand blender until well combined.

2. Line an 8×8-inch (20×20-cm) pan with parchment paper. Do this with two overlapping strips, leaving the corners bare. This is to avoid any crinkling of the paper which will cause uneven edges in the cake. Spray the parchment paper and any exposed pan (mostly in the corners) with cooking spray. Pour the cake batter in, and gently shake the pan to ensure an even cake.

3. Bake for 25 to 30 minutes, or until a toothpick runs clean after poking the middle of the cake. Remove from the oven and let it rest for 10 minutes, then carefully lift it out of the pan using the parchment paper and let it cool on a wire rack.

Assembly

1. So, there are few options for this. If making a cake like the photo is desired, make sure to double the cake recipe and bake in two 8×8-inch (20×20-cm) pans— or bake in one pan at separate times like I had to! Also, double the ice cream recipe as well! This will make a ton of cake and ice cream!

2. Once cakes have been baked, line the 8×8-inch (20×20-cm) pan with parchment paper and then pour in the ice cream after blending it a second time. Spread it so it's even on top. Freeze it for 1 to 2 hours, or until it's frozen through. Then, remove the ice cream from the pan, add one of the chocolate cakes back into the pan, then place the ice cream on top, and then place the second chocolate cake on top of that. Cut desired pieces, and top with hot fudge, vegan whipped cream, and a cherry!

3. Another option is to simply scoop out some ice cream and add that to a piece of cake, this is actually how the restaurant does it these days! The squared off ice cream is mostly for aesthetics. Additionally, it's possible to just have a single piece of cake with a scoop of ice cream and hot fudge, and it's still totally delicious! I've been eating the leftovers out of a coffee mug and it's probably my favorite thing! Top with some flaky salt, too!

WENDY'S FROSTY®

If you recently became vegan after being a longtime vegetarian, there's a good chance while everyone was ordering burgers you were ordering sides and one of these! Even though I didn't go to Dave's place nearly as much as I did others, I remember always getting this, even if it was late night and cold outside. If you're unfamiliar, there's also a tradition of dipping hot French fries in this concoction. Sound weird? Maybe. But there's something to be said for it, especially if you're a fan of sweet and salty.

YIELD: 4 SERVINGS

INGREDIENTS

Sweetened Condensed Milk

- 1 can (13.5 ounces, or 400 ml) full-fat coconut milk
- ⅓ cup (66 g) sugar, maple syrup, or agave
- 1 teaspoon vanilla extract

Chocolate Soft Serve

- 2 cups (475 ml) vegan chocolate milk
- 1 can (13.5 ounces, or 400 ml) full-fat coconut milk (chilled)
- ¼ cup (50 g) sugar, maple syrup, or agave
- 1 teaspoon vanilla extract

INSTRUCTIONS

Sweetened Condensed Milk

Add the ingredients to a medium-size saucepan over medium heat. Simmer and reduce to ½ cup (120 ml). Store it in a jar in the refrigerator. It will thicken a lot once cooled. It should be super sweet!

Chocolate Soft Serve

Freeze the chocolate milk in an ice cube tray for 6 hours or overnight. Chill the coconut milk in the top shelf of the refrigerator overnight as well. Only use the cream from the coconut milk, reserving the water for a smoothie or something else. Then, add everything to a high-speed blender and blitz until smooth. Serve immediately and enjoy!

NOTE: For a short cut, use canned vegan condensed milk.

NOTE: Don't have a high-speed blender? You can also use a hand or stand mixer.

DAIRY QUEEN OREO® BLIZZARD®

I haven't had too many of these in my lifetime, but my wife certainly has. This re-creation got her seal of approval, and you can even hold these upside down and they won't slip out—just like the real deal! Here we are making an Oreo-inspired flavor, but feel free to add any other mix-ins your heart desires.

YIELD: 4 SERVINGS

INGREDIENTS

Ice Cream

- ▶ 2 cans (13.5 ounces, or 400 ml each) full-fat coconut milk (chilled)
- ▶ ⅔ cup (230 g) agave
- ▶ 1 tablespoon (15 ml) vanilla extract
- ▶ Pinch of ground cinnamon
- ▶ Pinch of ground nutmeg
- ▶ Pinch of salt

Assembly

- ▶ 4–5 chocolate sandwich cookies, such as Oreos or Newman-Os, or more to taste

INSTRUCTIONS

Ice Cream

Chill the coconut milk on the top shelf of the refrigerator overnight. Only use the cream from the coconut milk, reserving the water for a smoothie or something else. Then, add all the ingredients to a high-speed blender and blend just until combined. Use a tamper if needed, but be careful not to over blend, which can cause the cream to curdle and separate. Chill in a freezer-proof container overnight. Let the ice cream thaw until slightly softened. While the ice cream thaws, add the bowl from a stand mixer to the freezer for 20 minutes.

Assembly

1. Crush the cookies either in a food processor or by adding them to a zip-top bag and crushing with a rolling pin.

2. Once the ice cream has partially thawed and the bowl is cold, add the ice cream to the bowl. Mix on medium-low speed until smooth and creamy. Gently fold in the crushed cookies. Serve immediately!

> **NOTE:** You can also use a hand mixer instead of a stand mixer, but don't use a high speed-blender as this will obliterate the cookies and ruin the texture (at least in my humble opinion!).

CHICK-FIL-A PEACH MILKSHAKE

This is a seasonal item only offered during the summer. And like just about everything at this restaurant, it's not vegan at all! Luckily, it's fairly easy to veganize this at home as the flavor is powered by the fruit. I wasn't part of the legion of fans that looks forward to this milkshake every year, but I can see why it's a summertime staple. I could enjoy this year-round! Why not pair this with a Chicken Sandwich (page 58) and get the full experience at home.

YIELD: 3 TO 4 SERVINGS

INGREDIENTS

- 2 cans (13.5 ounces, or 400 ml each) full-fat coconut milk (chilled)
- 2 cans (15 ounces, or 425 g each) peaches, drained
- ¾ cup (255 g) agave
- 1 tablespoon (15 ml) vanilla extract
- Vegan whipped cream for topping
- Cherries for topping

INSTRUCTIONS

1. Chill the coconut milk in the top shelf of the refrigerator overnight. Only use the cream from the coconut milk, reserving the water for a smoothie or something else. Then, mix everything in a high-speed blender, using a tamper if needed, and only blending until everything is combined. Be careful not to over blend, otherwise the cream might curdle and separate.

2. Once blended, serve immediately with some vegan whipped cream and a cherry. Store unblended leftovers for later and just blend it up before serving to get that classic milkshake consistency.

> **NOTE:** If your milkshake is too thick, just add 2 to 4 tablespoons (30 to 60 ml) of unsweetened plant milk at a time and blend until it reaches the desired consistency.

RESOURCES

Here are some of my favorite vegan products, websites, bloggers, and YouTubers! This is just a smattering. There's so much more out there, but this is a good starting point!

Products

▶ Follow Your Heart® makes my favorite vegan mayo (Vegenaise®). They also make some great vegan cheeses and salad dressings!

▶ So Delicious® has great cheeses and ice cream!

▶ Violife® also makes some of my favorite cheeses. I use the cheddar shreds quite often for the Easy Cheese Sauce!

▶ Kite Hill® makes my favorite vegan cream cheese and ricotta!

▶ Tofurky® makes some great vegan chick'n and deli meats!

▶ Gardein® makes a lot of convenient frozen foods, and the Lightly Seasoned Chick'n Scallopini is what I typically use for Fried Chick'n (see page 20).

▶ Beyond, Alpha Foods, and Impossible Meat all make great plant-based meats, including burgers, chicken nuggets, and sausages!

▶ All Vegetarian Inc. (they are vegan!) make some amazing vegan meats, and their bacon is my favorite store-bought bacon. You can buy from them online.

▶ The BE-Hive makes some amazing vegan meats as well!

▶ JUST Egg is super handy and useful!

▶ Ripple® is my favorite unsweetened plant milk.

▶ Bob's Red Mill has a lot of great products for baking.

▶ Modernist Pantry, Druid's Grove, and Spiceology are great for some of the more uncommon ingredients, such as lactic acid and sodium citrate.

▶ If you're in LA (or ever visiting) you gotta hit up BESTIES Vegan Paradise. It's an all-vegan market, and it's run by some really awesome folks! Plus, they carry a lot of items you can't find anywhere else!

Bloggers / YouTubers

These folks can be found on Instagram, YouTube, or the good old internet in blog form!

▶ Sauce Stache

▶ Eat Figs, Not Pigs

▶ Hot For Food

▶ The Edgy Veg

▶ Plantifully Based

▶ Turnip Vegan

▶ Avocadoes and Ales

▶ Ugly Vegan

▶ Zacchary Bird

▶ Vegan Hippie Sol

▶ Mary's Test Kitchen

▶ Chez Jorge

▶ Big Box Vegan

▶ 86 Eats

▶ Mississippi Vegan

▶ Avant Garde Vegan

▶ Nora Cooks

▶ PlantYou

ACKNOWLEDGMENTS

I want to thank my amazing wife, April, not only for being the one who urged me to start this whole thing, but for being super supportive and encouraging, and most especially for patiently listening to my never-ending stream of consciousness about burgers! I want to thank my parents and sister for always supporting me and all my weirdo interests and endeavors. Shout-out to my grandparents for taking me to Bob's Big Boy and showing me the joys of deep-fried homemade tacos.

Also hat tip to Ashley from Eat Figs, Not Pigs, Lauren from Hot for Food, and Carleigh Bodrug of PlantYou for bestowing me with their sage advice on writing a cookbook.

And lastly but not leastly, I want to thank everyone who's supported me throughout the years, especially those of you who have made some of my recipes and have let me know how much you enjoyed them. That really is one of the best parts of this whole thing, which is sharing something with y'all, and I just feel so dang lucky to be doing this, so thank you and I hope you're all doing well!

ABOUT THE AUTHOR

Brian Watson, aka Thee Burger Dude, went vegan in 2018. Since the moment the switch flipped, he's been busy veganizing his favorite foods as well as nostalgic dishes from childhood. Soon after starting an Instagram showcasing these meals, he received a ton of positive feedback, which quickly led to a blog and YouTube channel. Videos for everything from rice paper bacon to vegan burgers now log hundreds of thousands of views, delivering on his goal from the get-go: to help vegans and non-vegans alike make delicious, exciting dishes that are better for animals (and often better than the non-vegan originals!). Born and raised in Southern California, Brian currently resides in the lovely town of Burbank with his wife, April, and their cat, Pixel. Thee Burger Dude has been featured in *VegNews*, *Best of Vegan*, and many other vegan and non-vegan publications. You can find him online at theeburgerdude.com and on social media channels as "Thee Burger Dude."

INDEX